Critical Guides to French Texts

119 Scarron: Le Roman comique

Critical Guides to French Texts

EDITED BY ROGER LITTLE, WOLFGANG VAN EMDEN, DAVID WILLIAMS

SCARRON

Le Roman comique

Richard Parish

Professor of French, University of Oxford
and Fellow of St Catherine's College

Grant & Cutler Ltd
1998

© Grant & Cutler Ltd 1998
ISBN 0 7293 0405 1

T 1001512509

DEPÓSITO LEGAL: V. 4.018 - 1998

Printed in Spain by
Artes Gráficas Soler, S.A., Valencia
for
GRANT & CUTLER LTD
55-57 GREAT MARLBOROUGH STREET, LONDON W1V 2AY

Contents

for my colleagues

Bruce, Robert and Colin

Acknowledgements

I should like to acknowledge my gratitude to the editors of *Seventeenth-Century French Studies* for granting permission to reproduce parts of an article published in that journal. It also gives me pleasure to thank Dr Elfrieda Dubois for so generously lending me her flat in the Yvelines, where much of this study was written; and Dr Nicholas Cronk, who read and commented on an earlier draft.

Prefatory Note

The *Roman comique* is constituted by two parts of a (conjecturally) projected tripartite structure, the first dating from 1651, the second from 1657. Scarron died before he could finish writing, but an anonymous third part was added in 1663 (the so-called *Suite d'Offray*), and the first edition of the three parts appeared in 1678, in the same year as *La Princesse de Clèves*. I shall devote some attention in Appendix I to this as to other attempts to continue and indeed finish the work; however, as it is generally acknowledged that, whatever their independent interest, they add little to the extant authentic books, I shall limit my remarks in the bulk of the argument to these.

Page references are to the edition by Yves Giraud (Garnier-Flammarion, 1981); however students will find the edition of Jean Serroy (Folio, 1985) equally cheap and convenient. Spelling is modernized in both. Serroy includes some information about and summaries of the various attempts to continue or complete the novel; the earlier 'Classiques Garnier' edition reproduces the *Suite d'Offray in toto*.

Italicized numbers in parentheses, followed where appropriate by a page reference, refer to the numbered items in the Selected Bibliography at the end of this volume.

Since there is a wide range of contemporary literary reference in the text, I have felt obliged to reflect this in my critical remarks, and indeed on occasion to extend it. I have therefore marked the names of writers (and anonymous works) with an asterisk (*) at the first occurrence, and provided a brief explanatory gloss in Appendix II.

I have modernized spelling throughout of texts from the seventeenth century and later; however I have maintained the original spelling in quotations from Rabelais.

1. The Literary Context

Background and genre

> *L'Histoire comique* de M. Scarron [...] décrit la vie de quelques comédiens et d'autres gens de toutes conditions, avec des naïvetés incomparables, et il leur arrive à tous de fort plaisantes aventures. Cela est d'un style particulier à l'auteur, qui est de faire raillerie de tout, même dans les narrations où il parle lui-même, ce qui est proprement le style burlesque plutôt que le comique. Néanmoins toutes les pièces qui composent ce roman étant fort diverses, on a peine à juger de son ordre, et de sa juste liaison, et de son principal sujet, à cause qu'il n'est point achevé. (*15*, p.59 [p.199])

The French seventeenth century is too easily perceived as an age of monolithic literary certainties: dominated on the stage by Corneille*, Molière* and Racine*; marked by the intellectual authority of Descartes* and Pascal*; redolent of the *salons*, whose spirit is encapsulated in the writings of La Rochefoucauld*, La Bruyère* or Sévigné*; above all, an aristocratic age of elegance, decorum and order. A limited study such as this one can not do more than begin to challenge that view; but by concentrating on a work which perpetually pulls the reader between a sense of control and its (often violent) disruption, which is unfinished and heterogeneous, and whose subject-matter is drawn from the humblest of milieux, that of travelling players, we are bound to throw into question certain fixed preconceptions about the century of classicism.

The study of a novel compounds our need for reappraisal. The novel, of all the major genres in the period, is the least known, with the exception of the one masterpiece of La Fayette*, *La Princesse de Clèves* (1678), and in some respects the least accessible. If, as I hope to show, Scarron's *Roman comique* is among the most enjoyable of

the literary creations of the French seventeenth century, both it and
its companions in the genre have been largely neglected by critics
until recent years. Before turning to my central text, therefore, I shall
briefly survey the range of writing which constitutes the genre of the
novel, and particularly the sub-genre of the comic novel in the
period, before going on to explore some of the many reasons why we
might legitimately take an interest in what has, in some respects,
tended to be considered as a relatively minor literary phenomenon.

If the comic novel forms a distinct strand in contemporary
narrative fiction, it remains acutely and critically conscious of the
pastoral and heroic traditions which flourished in the first half of the
century, successors in turn to the chivalric romance. The most
famous of these was Honoré d'Urfé's* digressive pastoral, *L'Astrée*,
which appeared between 1607 and 1627 but which, for all its 4,000
pages, was left unfinished by its author. (In some respects, the
question of finishing is an irrelevance – as it will be for the *Roman
comique* – since both traditions place their major focus of interest in
the episodes which constitute the bulk of the narrative, rather than in
any purposeful movement towards a resolution. There is no more
obvious reason why *L'Astrée* or the *Roman comique* should be
'finished' than why *Coronation Street* should be.) *L'Astrée* is set in
fifth-century Gaul, and concerns the love of a shepherd and a
shepherdess, but uses this pretext essentially as a framework for a
vast number of sentimental digressions, the most famous of which
concern the hero Céladon's protracted disguise as a woman (an
element which is, however, treated without any degree of comic
awareness). The later serious development of the genre takes the
form of the heroic or epic novel, of which the most celebrated
examples are Gomberville's* exotic *Polexandre* (1619-37), La
Calprenède's* *Cassandre* (1642-45) and *Cléopâtre* (1646-57), and
above all Madeleine de Scudéry's* *Le Grand Cyrus* (1649-53) and
Clélie (1654-60). Here the setting is recent history (*Polexandre*) or
classical antiquity; and these vast plot-driven novels are
characterized by complexity, digression, hyperbole, coincidence,
exhaustiveness and, progressively, by a didactic and moralizing
purpose.

Parodic reference, both explicit and implicit, to these traditions is present in much of the comic writing of the period, including Scarron's *Roman comique*, which 'shares with other realistic novels [...] a highly critical attitude towards the heroic and sentimental novels that proliferate in the wake of d'Urfé' (*45*, p.131). Before looking briefly at the major serious manifestation of the genre later in the period, therefore, it is to two other examples of comic writing in the earlier part of the century that I shall attend: the *Vraie histoire comique de Francion* of Sorel* and Furetière's* *Roman bourgeois*.

Sorel's novel presents us with the greatest difficulties insofar as the status of the text is concerned. It was originally published in a six-book version, of which the final book was divided, in 1623. Four further books were later added, and an eleven-book second edition was published in 1626, before a final twelfth book completed the project in 1633. All parts of the novel are by Sorel, and there would be a *prima facie* logic in taking the final version as definitive. However a problem arises from the fact that the twelve-book version incorporates a significant reworking of the earlier chapters, much of whose audacity is consequently lost. Structurally, on the other hand, the twelve-book version is increasingly taken as offering the greatest degree of coherence, since the first seven books narrate the (mostly amorous) adventures of the hero, Francion, up to the point at which he sees the portrait of his ideal woman, Naïs, whose pursuit then forms the subject of the remaining chapters, leading to the couple's marriage in Italy at the work's conclusion. The sense is thus conveyed of a maturing in the hero, after his licentious youthful escapades, and a final triumph of idealized love. The episodic narrative progression to the dénouement is however immensely complex and eventful, an impression reinforced by the fact that the whole novel begins *in medias res*, and only reaches the present moment of narration at the end of the sixth book.

Francion is most of all remarkable for its bawdy good humour, and represents, in its first edition at least, by far the most superficially daring of the three principal comic prose texts of the period. Yet this quality is combined, paradoxically, with a strong element of idealism, and the eponymous hero, who moves through a great diversity of social strata, encapsulates in so doing a kind of free-spirited hedonism that is unique in the genre. All of the comic novels in the period are episodic, but only here is it possible to suggest that this feature is inherent to the theme and, in particular, to the philosophy of the work, to which Coulet accords the status of 'une rhapsodie' (*20*, p.193). *Francion*'s most famous moment is known as the 'épisode des généreux', and concerns a band of students, 'personnes toutes braves et ennemies de la sottise et de l'ignorance', united 'pour converser ensemblement, et faire une infinité de gentillesses' (*6*, p.250); and even after the dissolution of what is clearly a transient and to some degree élitist company, Francion's principle in life remains to 'châtier les sottises, de rabaisser les vanités et de me moquer de l'ignorance des hommes' (*6*, pp.261-62). Coexisting with such idealism, we find the account of all kinds of debauchery and excess, culminating in a hedonistic episode known as the 'fête chez Raymond', which critics generally consider to constitute the turning point in the novel. Most striking of all is the treatment of physical love, represented as 'une sorte de force élémentaire qui domine l'homme et le fait participer à la vie universelle' (*16*, p.64). It exists in a climate that is free from morality, and thus free from guilt. The purely comic dimension to the work, alongside the tumultuous succession of adventures, is frequently erotic or scatological, and makes extensive use, as will the *Roman comique*, of the techniques commonly associated with stage farce. The understanding of comedy in this text is thus dominated by licentiousness and yet, even in its earliest version, the work is not without a kind of subversive moral purpose. Neither of those aspects will be central to, or perhaps even present in the later novels.

The second of the companion texts within the comic sub-genre is the *Roman bourgeois* of Furetière, dating from 1666. Here we are dealing with a text that offers no external bibliographical problems, but which, although finished, deliberately presents the most bewildering structure of all three novels: 'C'est [...] un défi total que lance Furetière aux lois externes et internes du genre tel qu'il avait été pratiqué jusqu'à lui' (*7*, p.7). Although formally the work consists of two books, there is little or no narrative link between them, and the *Au Lecteur* in fact occurs before the second. Digression around a series of loose thematic links is the apparent compositional principle of the work, and the episodes are indeed connected by some structural similarities; but whereas digressions are a feature of most fictional works of the period, they are, in the case of the *Roman bourgeois*, the whole of the novel. There is a novelistic infrastructure without a superstructure, and the work's last section charts its own disintegration in a succession of lists of ever-increasing specificity. These features furthermore function within a persistent denial of novelistic conventions (be they invention, omniscience or an ordering purpose), so that an anti-novel is being written alongside the conventional novel that is being parodied or subverted. Finally, the characters whom Furetière portrays, drawn from the legal milieux of Paris, are presented with virtually no redeeming features; they are, for the first time in the history of the genre, offered as thoroughly mediocre and, as such, are ridiculed by the narrator. In this way, the work is both *anti-roman* and also *anti-bourgeois*; indeed one is part and parcel of the other, as Furetière parodies the *romanesque*, yet despises its alternative. As Coulet concludes, the *Roman bourgeois* remains '[une] œuvre marquante dans l'histoire du genre romanesque [...], instructive par son échec même' (*20*, p.277).

Looking now further forward, and returning to the more serious manifestations of the genre, we reach its most universally recognized masterpiece in the period, *La Princesse de Clèves*, written by the Comtesse de La Fayette, and published in 1678. Here we have a work that is relatively brief, yet complete, and whose four digressions, all occurring in the first half of the novel, nevertheless relate closely to the central narrative. The work, which begins with an evocation of the court of Henri II, and ends with a spotlight on the isolated figure of the heroine in the years leading to her death, tells a tautly-written story of the drama of illicit passion in a recent historical setting, and poses, without answering them, some of the most fundamental questions concerning self-knowledge, personal motivation and individual responsibility. The superficially limpid style of narration nonetheless conceals a turbulent psychological investigation worked out against an ethically anarchic backdrop, and represents an abandonment of any previous understanding of the *romanesque* in favour of a plausible, albeit elevated, account of a universal dilemma. Whereas I shall go on to suggest certain (superficially improbable) parallels between our principal text and the classical perfection of its most famous successor, it might also be appropriate to quote Lever in suggesting the role of Furetière's anti-novel in effecting a transition: 'Ce n'est pas tout à fait un hasard si le *Roman bourgeois* se situe au seuil de l'âge classique', he writes. 'S'il ne l'annonce d'aucune manière, du moins fait-il allègrement table rase de ce qui l'a précédé' (*26*, p.164).

If the comic novels relate however distantly to the broader evolution of the French novel of the period, they also relate extensively both internationally and chronologically. The tradition to which they look outside France is predominantly Spanish, reflecting a fashion which began with the translation into French of the first picaresque novel, *Lazarillo de Tormes**, in 1561, and which continued into the mid-seventeenth century. The degree to which Sorel's *Francion* and Scarron's *Roman comique* are indebted to this tradition is contested, but certain picaresque features, notably that of a travelling framework of some description, loosely tying together a series of episodes, are undeniably identifiable in both, even if the specifics of the tradition, in particular the humble origins of the roguish protagonist (the *pícaro*), are not respected in the case of *Francion*. As De Armas remarks, 'the genre as a whole was more important in the genesis of the *Roman comique* than any specific picaresque novel' (*36*, p.57). Secondly, and crucially, Cervantes's* *Don Quijote* was translated into French in 1614, and is the most frequently quoted Spanish intertext for the *Roman comique*, as well as an inspiration to practitioners of novelistic subversion for centuries to come. There is an extended comparison in the first interpolated story: 'S'il eût été de l'humeur de dom Quichotte, il eût [...]' (p.95), alongside two of its own Spanish precursors (thus plunging the reference chronologically backwards), as well as a heated discussion in the argument between Roquebrune and La Garouffière (I, xxi), to which we shall return in some detail. Most specifically, the Spanish masterpiece is reflected in the use of often parodic chapter titles, and of interpolated shorter narrations (*novelas cortas* [*nouvelles*]). The same writer's equally influential *Novelas ejemplares* were translated into French in 1615 (see *23*). Finally, *El Viaje entretenido* of Agustín de Rojas*, of 1603, is equally a clear, if a very different precursor of the *Roman comique* itself, devoted as it is to the account of a journey through Spain by Rojas and three theatrical associates, and involving as it does the occasional description of a dramatic performance. Yet here again, 'there are no parallels between any specific events' (*36*, p.58), and it already says something about all of the comic novels in the period that none of them is a direct imitation, and none is directly imitated. They are heterogeneous as a group as well as being tonally diverse within individual examples.

Looking now at the novels with reference to the French intertexts, we see the strand of writing looking back most saliently to Rabelais*, whose incomplete *chroniques* (there are four authenticated books) devoted to the adventures of the giants Gargantua and Pantagruel, and notorious for their scatology and verbal excesses, are clearly related both linguistically and philosophically to Sorel's *Francion* as well as furnishing echoes in Scarron's work. Reminders are also present of the tradition of the sixteenth-century *conteurs*, and similarities of tone and structure are frequent with the writing of Marguerite de Navarre*, whose *Heptaméron* is in turn an imitation of Boccaccio's* *Decameron*. In particular the existence of independent narratives within a framework creates a link between the Boccaccian tradition and the *Roman comique*, even though the later work has none of the moralizing or indeed theological elements which are to some degree implicit in the original and explicit in its French imitator. What loosely unites our novels with the French, Spanish and Italian models that they either parody or imitate is an exploitation of the technique of digressions within a framework.

The comic novels relate as well to other areas of writing and, for want of a better word, movements, in the period. There are striking connexions with the theatre and with satire; and the sub-

genre attracts to itself, and thus helps to define, certain notorious
terms of both contemporary and later criticism: *burlesque*; *romanesque*; baroque; classical. But in addition to this, it poses problems as
to its own genre. As E. M. Forster remarked: 'The novel, in my view,
has not any rules, and so there is no such thing as the art of fiction'
(*22*, p.183), a comment that would apply particularly well to our text
and certain of its close relations. Furthermore, if the word 'roman'
means different things, so does the word 'comique': in the case of
Francion, we may identify a meaning that has associations of broad
comedy in the spirit of *libertinage*; in the *Roman comique* itself we
encounter the dominant theatrical overtones, to which we shall return
at length; and in the later *Roman bourgeois*, subtitled 'Ouvrage
comique', these are both largely replaced by the concept of a self-
subversive narrative. As Serroy writes, in fact of *Francion*, but
applicably more broadly to the whole sub-genre: 'On hésite à [les]
classer dans telle ou telle catégorie romanesque' (*32*, p.124).

One possible definition of the sub-genre is however provided
in the period by one of the novelists, and is found in Sorel's
Bibliothèque françoise:

> On parle des romans comiques en général, mais on les
> divise aussi en satiriques et en burlesques, et quelques-
> uns sont tout cela ensemble. Les bons romans comiques
> et satiriques semblent plutôt être des images de l'histoire
> que tous les autres. Les actions communes de la vie étant
> leur objet, il est plus facile d'y rencontrer de la vérité.
> Pour ce qu'on voit plus d'hommes dans l'erreur et dans
> la sottise qu'il y en a de portés à la sagesse, il se trouve
> parmi eux plus d'occasions de raillerie, et leur défauts ne
> produisent que la satire. [...] On rencontre là plutôt le
> genre vraisemblable que dans les pièces héroïques qui ne
> sont que fiction, puisqu'il y a peu d'hommes qui méritent
> d'être estimés des héros, c'est-à-dire quelque chose entre
> les dieux et les hommes. (*15*, p.57 [pp.188-9])

As Serroy comments: 'Le roman perd le caractère de fiction extraordinaire qu'il avait dans la veine héroïque. Il se penche désormais non pas sur des héros, mais sur des hommes' (*32*, p.120). The absence of classically distanced figures is indeed a common feature, as is the presence of parodied ones; but if the degree of ridicule of folly is both high and consistent, the degree of ordinariness is variable, and it will not really be until Furetière's *Roman bourgeois* of 1666 that genuinely mediocre figures are central to the narrative: 'le vrai roman réaliste du xviie siècle, c'est le *Roman bourgeois* et non le *Roman comique*' (*2*, p.36). In the *Avertissement* to his later novel *Polyandre* (1648), Sorel goes on to stress the moral aspects of the sub-genre but, here again, it would be difficult to apply such a criterion to all (some would say any) of the works concerned. Novelty, amusement and variety all seem to be common features, and perhaps the only definition that will suffice is a very simple one, such as that provided at the beginning of the first chapter of the third (1633) and subsequent editions of *Francion*: 'Nous avons assez d'histoires tragiques qui ne font que nous attrister. Il en faut maintenant voir une qui soit toute comique, et qui puisse apporter de la délectation aux esprits les plus ennuyés' (*6*, p.378).

Closely related to this question of definition is the use of the terms '*anti-roman*' and 'anti-novel'. Lever makes a useful general point pertinent to the text we shall study more closely, when he writes that 'la peinture de la vie quotidienne contient presque toujours, au xviie siècle, une dérision implicite de l'esprit romanesque. En ce sens, on peut considérer toute histoire comique comme un *anti-roman*' (*26*, pp.93-94). He then goes on to provide a definition of the term, proposing that the process of writing the anti-novel is characterized in the period by the effort to 'dénoncer l'illusion par le biais d'une autre illusion' (*26*, p.94). Adam suggests that the *Roman bourgeois* is an anti-novel, but that the *Roman comique* is not (*1*, pp.38; 46); and Giraud in his introduction to the text is as specific as to say that *Francion* is 'une anti-Astrée' (*6*, p.16). There are also contemporary parodies of individual works: Scarron produced one such in his *Virgile travesti* of 1648-51; and Sorel wrote a specific parody of *L'Astrée* in 1627, entitled *Le Berger extravagant*, to which the explicit alternative title of *L'Anti-Roman* was added in 1633. Clearly inspired by *Don Quijote* in its treatment of literary delusion, it charts the progress of a hero with pastoral aspirations through a series of exaggeratedly bucolic adventures. The novel's subtitle further stresses the theoretical critique (it is a story 'où parmi des fantaisies amoureuses on voit les impertinences des romans et de la poésie'), as does Sorel's stated intention to 'composer un livre qui se moquât des autres et qui fût comme le tombeau des romans' (*14*, preface [non-paginated]), an aim which will in fact come close to being realized by Furetière.

Comic novels take us in addition, socially and linguistically, into areas which are little represented in the canonical writers of the time (with the salient exceptions of letters and memoirs). By the very nature of its authorship and patronage, the greater part of French seventeenth-century prose writing is centred on Paris and the court, yet more modest milieux find unparalleled fictional exploitation in all works in the sub-genre: the world of college life is extensively described in *Francion*; that of a provincial theatrical troupe in the *Roman comique*; and that of the legal profession in the *Roman bourgeois*. But equally all are situated within a remarkably broad social context. It is obviously not very fruitful to read such works simply for snippets of historical information, insight or *pittoresque*, but at the same time we do well to be alerted to this element in the writing, not just because of its relative rarity, but also because of its capacity to allow the writers concerned their maximum descriptive freedom and vigour. The milieux they write about are those they know and thus represent most effectively, even if that very proximity may on occasion introduce a degree of caricatural myopia. Linguistically, too, the vernacular lexicon in all three novels may remind us more of the freedom of sixteenth-century usage than of the rigour of the seventeenth; and certainly in *Francion* we are often closer to the language of Rabelais than to that of Racine.

Finally, from a different critical angle again, all works represent considerable interest from the point of view of order and / or disorganization. A mixture of chance and deliberateness produces particularly complicated structural problems; and it is neither interesting nor accurate to suggest that these all stem from simple carelessness. These novels lend themselves to a variety of types of reading: they are open texts, exhibiting a *prima facie* randomness of structure, sometimes seeking to play on several narrative levels at once; yet showing an awareness of the conventions of formal composition, in which their freedom is apparently grounded. Such experimentation again looks back to the first traces of novelistic self-consciousness in early modern France in Bonaventure des Périer's* *Nouvelles Récréations* (1558) or outside France in Cervantes; and forwards to Diderot's* *Jacques le fataliste* (1796), to Gide's* *Les Faux-Monnayeurs* (1926) and ultimately to the *nouveau roman**. It might indeed seem tempting to record a pattern of subversion and re-creation in the history of the French novel as a whole[1]. Certainly, the strongest impression created is one of definition by contrast and negation, as Scarron's work demonstrates as well as any.

The literary in the text

Within this framework, a high degree of literary awareness informs the whole text of the *Roman comique*. The business of literary creation is given its first substantial, if parodic treatment upon the introduction of the loosely attached poet, Roquebrune, in I, viii, tolerated as an actor only in minor roles and a butt of comic attention on account of his unfulfilled artistic pretentions. Yet animated literary discussion follows in the same chapter, even if it is immediately parodied by the narrator on account of its transparent name-dropping: 'Le poète [...] se tuait de leur dire qu'il avait vu Corneille, qu'il avait fait la débauche avec Saint-Amant* et Beys* et qu'il avait perdu un bon ami en feu Rotrou*' (p.84-85). And at the end of the same chapter, Ragotin's dramatic aspirations are given

---

[1] Waugh remarks in her study of 'the theory and practice of self-conscious literature' (*Metafiction*) that 'ultimately questions about the viability of metafiction lead to questions about the viability of the novel itself and its possible future developments' (*33*, p.63). Although she writes predominantly about modern novelists (and Scarron is not even mentioned), many of her points are nonetheless remarkably pertinent to our text, and I shall therefore introduce them as and when they seem germane to the argument.

equally short shrift, preluding a motivic use of the comic couple's mutual inadequacies. Soon thereafter (I, x), we learn that Ragotin wishes for a comedy to be made out of his story, but is thwarted in his aims; Le Destin painstakingly explains to him the reasons for its unsuitability; and there follows a dispute in which Le Destin's reasonable objections meet outrageously irrelevant counterpoints. It only takes La Rancune to side with Ragotin for the argument to be reduced to hilarity ('Ce bel expédient [...] de La Rancune fit rire toute la compagnie', p.106); nevertheless in both the semi-serious initial discussion of *bienséances* between Le Destin and Ragotin and in the succession of laughable parallels which ensues, matters of both aesthetic principles and feasibility are comically aired within a modest framework of generic awareness and contemporary theatrical reference.

More sustained attention is given at two points in the novel to the defence of the two artistic domains it encompasses (the novel itself and the theatre). The first passage to consider in this light occurs in the story of Le Destin, whose education in the library of the baron d'Arques had consisted of reading novels, since 'la lecture des bons romans instruisait en divertissant et [d'Arques] ne les croyait pas moins propres à donner de beaux sentiments aux jeunes gens que la lecture de Plutarque*' (p.121). Such an opinion, vouchsafed to a figure of such obvious, if shadowy, generosity and couched in terms of contemporary requirements of good taste, thus lends support to the genre as a whole. The young Le Destin then devotes his free time to the reading of novels; and, although he finds chivalric romances more to his taste at that stage, he eventually progresses to those later pastoral manifestations (such as *L'Astrée*) by which 'les Français ont fait voir, aussi bien que par mille autres choses, que, s'ils n'inventent pas tant que les autres nations, ils perfectionnent davantage' (ibid.). Since the novel, no less than the theatre, had its critics in certain right-thinking milieux of the period, so Scarron's work acts indirectly, by the young actor's defence of the genre, as an implicit apologia for the literary activity it exemplifies.

Alongside the implicit defence of the novel, a more explicit effort in the direction of an apologia for the theatre is attempted in an important passage in II, viii, entitled 'Ce qui arriva au pied de Ragotin' (but which is not principally about this subject at all). Here the social desirability of actors is stressed, and the narrator remarks that 'de nos jours on a rendu en quelque façon justice à leur profession et on les estime plus que l'on ne faisait autrefois' (p.249). The theatre ['la comédie'] has furthermore, he claims, been 'purgée, au moins à Paris, de tout ce qu'elle avait de licencieux', with the result that 'le peuple trouve un divertissement des plus innocents et qui peut à la fois instruire et plaire' (ibid.). The narrator seems to be sincere in his praise here at least, given his generally sympathetic attitude towards the subjects of his account; and no doubt reflects a genuine evolution in taste in his apparently rather puritanical defence of the propriety of the theatre of his day.

The critically most important chapter (I, xxi), containing the most sustained literary debate of the novel (despite being entitled 'Qui peut-être ne sera pas trouvé fort divertissant') is endowed with a multiple function. The views of the 'jeune conseiller de Rennes' on the theatre, and in particular on the neoclassical unities, whilst initially appearing iconoclastic, rapidly become more moderate, concluding as he does that 'l'on pourrait faire des pièces qui seraient fort bien reçues sans tomber dans les extravagances des Espagnols et sans se géhenner par la rigueur des règles d'Aristote*' (p.184). Moving on to the novel, he offers a strong defence of the Spanish *nouvelles*, including a specific reference to Cervantes, and in preference to the contemporary French heroic novel. The defence of the latter (and attacks on *Don Quijote*), by being vouchsafed to Roquebrune, are thereby subverted. The essential function is thus to foreground a discussion of literary taste; but inevitably, given the spokesmen for the various positions, and given that a Spanish *nouvelle* constitutes the following chapter, some promotion of that sub-genre (and implicit demotion of the French heroic tendency) must emerge as the strongest argument.

More specific attention is also given, here and elsewhere, to contemporary prose fiction, notably to its excessive length; and it is by exaggerating this dimension that the point is made. *Cyrus* is mentioned in passing in I, xii, to the effect that the novel being written would never differ from the first impressions it creates on the reader, 'quand le livre serait aussi gros que le *Cyrus*' (p.111 – Scudéry's novel reaches some 8,500 pages); and again in the discussion which takes place during I, xxi, alongside the novels of Gomberville and La Calprenède: 'Roquebrune [...] ne promettait pas moins que de faire un roman en cinq parties, chacune de dix volumes, qui effacerait les *Cassandre*, *Cléopâtre*, *Polexandre* et *Cyrus*' (p.185). However, as Coulet accurately notes, Scarron, unlike Sorel, 'ne veut pas faire une parodie systématique, il se contente de quelques pointes' (*20*, p.202).

The remaining element to consider concerns the explicit treatment of contemporary theatrical writing, which points as well towards the changing tastes of the period. The major tragic playwright of the sixteenth century, Robert Garnier*, figures in the account of the performance of his *[Roger et] Bradamante* (1582), appropriately enough in the section related by La Caverne recounting her youth (p.223). In this way the chronology of theatrical performance is accurately reflected, even if the burden of the story is the incompetence of 'le grand page' in misremembering his single couplet. Alexandre Hardy*, the prolific playwright of the turn of the century, comes off badly, as we read of '*[le] temps qu'on* était réduit aux pièces de Hardy' (p.74, my emphasis), and of how he is no longer talked about. This is then reinforced by a repetition of the same phrase (*'du temps qu'on* en [trios] chantait') conveying a sense of a theatrical renaissance, or at the very least a rejection of the traditions of the recent past. Furthermore there is little doubt that one of the clearest literary *clefs*[2] in the text is contained in the work proposed for performance by Ragotin, the *Faits et gestes de Charlemagne, en vingt-quatre journées* (p.86), a parody of one of Hardy's tragi-comedies, *Les Chastes et Loyales Amours de Théagène et Chariclée* (1623-28), which was to be performed in eight

---

[2] The question of biographical *clefs* is addressed by H. Chardon in his *Scarron inconnu et les types des personnages du 'Roman comique'*, 2 vols, Paris, Champion, 1903-04. I would simply endorse Bénac's view of this activity, to the effect that 'ce qu'il nous apprend ne nous explique guère la physionomie romanesque que leur a donnée Scarron' (*2*, p.29).

'journées' each composed of five acts. Mention is made on a couple of occasions, both in a comic context, of Théophile de Viau's* *Pyrame et Thisbé* (first performed 1617, pp.106, 219); and a performance is initiated at the work's outset of Tristan L'Hermite's* tragedy *La Marianne* (1636, p.69) but, as will so often be the case, it is interrupted by a brawl. Moving closer to the period represented by the *Roman comique* itself, Corneille comes off rather better, and indeed his *Nicomède* (1651) is both praised and performed at the end of the novel (p.317); and L'Etoile's interpretation of the role of Chimène (from Corneille's tragi-comedy *Le Cid*) causes La Rappinière to fall in love with her (p.178). Finally Scarron is himself mentioned elliptically by reference to the best known of his comedies, *Dom Japhet* (1653), 'ouvrage de théâtre aussi enjoué que celui qui l'a fait a sujet de l'être peu' (p.314). It seems particularly appropriate that, once the troupe has reassembled in Le Mans, it marks its return by a performance of a play written by its creator, even if his most consistent comic creation, Ragotin, in turn (and predictably) brings about its interruption.

More minor literary references are made in passing, such as when an extract from a poem by Malherbe* is incorporated by (presumably) the primary narrator in a sententious capacity into the first interpolated story (p.96); then, after the 'opérateur' and his wife arrive in I, xv, and all are at table, the conversation turns briefly to the poetry of Théophile [de Viau] (p.138), and for once a dispute is averted. Elsewhere, technical terms are introduced and explained, such as when L'Etoile is described in a pretentious provincial literary context as being 'étourdie de quantité d'équivoques qu'on appelle pointes dans les provinces' (p.85); and the reader is expected to be able to pick up an unelaborated reference to 'le plus grand petit fou qui ait couru les champs depuis Roland' (Ariosto's* *Orlando Furioso*) at the first mention of Ragotin (p.86). Bringing several themes together, the ridiculing of the bad verse of Roquebrune (I, xii) initiates a violent dispute, thereby linking literary parody with the dominant physicality of the narrative, even if it is almost lost in the frenzied account of the conflict.

What emerges from our first examination of the *Roman comique* is that it contains scattered throughout a variety of literary debates alongside contemporary references and jibes (more often than not in chapters with titles such as 'Qui ne contient pas grand-chose'), all of which contribute to our view of the changing tastes of the period by providing 'une histoire discontinue de la littérature de jadis et de son temps' (*38*, p.329). It is a self-consciously literary piece of writing, in which all kinds of contemporary allusion accompany a high degree of formal awareness. Yet that element of literary sophistication permeates a text whose ostensible subject-matter and style might be thought to afford little such potential; and it is to these that we shall now attend.

2. The Troupe and the Theatre

The title of Scarron's novel contains an obvious pun: the novel is about actors; and it is funny; and these two meanings will indicate the substance of my next two chapters. Superficially, the *Roman comique* is concerned with the theatre, or more accurately with a group of travelling players; and such a company provides the ideal subject for an episodic narrative: 'Le comédien est instable et protéiforme par vocation; Scarron en fait un être hybride, à la fois héros de roman et acteur aux masques multiples. C'est peu de dire qu'il est mobile, il est le mouvement même' (*26*, p.153). They journey therefore – they are at Le Mans, and have come from Tours (an outbreak of the plague has prevented them from going on to Alençon) – and their sojourn of four or five days can be seen as indicating approximately the time scale of the work on the primary narrative level. Movement is not however limited to the vigorous opening description of their entry into Le Mans, rather the whole novel abounds in arrivals, departures and (often brutally interrupted) journeys; and, in the opening chapters of the second part in particular, the search for Angélique involves a great deal of displacement, albeit within a relatively small area. If no consistent destination is proposed, a sense of return is strongly created towards the end of the second part, as the troupe reassembles in Le Mans after its wanderings during the greater part of the book. This is already anticipated in II, xiii: 'Ils se trouvèrent alors dans le grand chemin du Mans et pressèrent leurs bêtes plus fort qu'ils n'avaient fait encore pour gagner un bourg qu'ils voyaient devant eux' (p.269), until at the end: 'On se coucha de bonne heure dans l'hôtellerie et, dès la pointe du jour, Le Destin et Léandre, chacun sa maîtresse en croupe, prirent le chemin du Mans où Ragotin, La Rancune et L'Olive étaient déjà retournés' (p.303), and where the reunited troupe finds relative security under its new patron, the marquis d'Orsé (II, vii). The business of travelling is not what primarily interests us, however, rather the past and present stories of the actors which constitute two of the major narrative strands of the text; yet the ability to capture the day-to-day provincial life of the troupe affords a central element of the novel's ethos, since 'the traveling actors' life partakes of the visionary splendors and romantic idealism of the artistic imagination and of the sordidness of an uncertain material existence' (*45*, p.135).

The troupe emerges as a cohesive unit, albeit a loose one, characterized by a spirit of equality and of confraternity: 'malgré la diversité de leurs origines sociales, ils forment une famille relativement unie et vivent entre eux sur le pied d'une parfaite égalité, se partageant les misères et les joies de leur aventureuse destinée' (*26*, p.153). The familial parallel is explicit in such remarks as 'La Caverne l'aimait [Le Destin] comme son propre fils; mademoiselle de L'Etoile ne lui était pas moins chère; et Angélique, sa fille et son unique héritière, aimait Le Destin et la L'Etoile comme son frère et sa sœur' (p.112), and Le Destin's later promise to Léandre: '"je vivrai avec vous comme avec un frère"' (p.235). The unit is assembled early in the novel and, although characters are detached from it or attached to it, survives until the end; it is depicted as being friendly and welcoming, and so acts magnetically, taking a host of fellow-travellers on board at various stages. The existence of this accretive nexus contributes to the facility with which Scarron introduces new characters into his work, complementing in this respect the setting of the various hostelries with their own arrivals and departures: initially the novel's primary episodes are centred on a hostelry in Le Mans, before moving to a second establishment, 'une assez bonne hôtellerie, parce qu'elle était sur le grand chemin' (p.229), for the majority of incidents in the earlier chapters of the second part.

Alongside mobility and flexibility, a further concomitant of the choice of subject matter is to create a novelistic milieu which does not foreground a single focal hero, but a composite one, a point which the author persona makes in I, v:

...il n'y en aura pas pour un [héros] dans ce livre-ci; et puisqu'il n'y a rien de plus parfait qu'un héros de livre, demi-douzaine de héros ou soi-disant tels feront plus d'honneur au mien qu'un seul qui serait peut-être celui dont on parlerait le moins... (p.74).

If there is not a single hero, Ragotin is no doubt the one character on whom Scarron depends most for his comic effects, and in I, xx, after a characteristic episode, the author persona concedes an awareness of his indispensability: '[J'étais] obligé en conscience de le tirer vitement du péril où il se trouve; car nous en aurons beaucoup à faire tandis que notre troupe comique sera dans la ville du Mans' (p.182); and Coulet notes that 'Ragotin est défini une fois pour toutes dès son entrée en scène' (*20*, p.204). Scarron uses him with ease; he is the most autonomous character, and so the character who by his flexibility is most appropriately involved in a diversity of comic episodes, almost invariably in the role of victim. He is the archetypal butt of misfortune, beginning with his unremovable hat in I, x, reflected (almost literally) in the unremovable chamber-pot of II, vii-viii, and affords a caricature of a grotesque brilliance. In addition he is periodically used in combination with La Rancune as a comedy double act, such as in I, xi, a fundamentally simple episode, all hot air and drink, yet sharply and cumulatively told. A balance is nonetheless kept between the individual and the troupe by making such figures into characters exclusively of the present, with none of the *romanesque* past of their new-found companions. Rather 'Ragotin, with his diminutive stature and ineffectual pugnacity, embodies a parody of the traditional hero of romance' (*45*, p.132); and, in this way, he is allowed to retain a proportionate status in the company, and in the novel, as a whole.

Alongside the comic hero is the brave hero, Le Destin, handsome, a good swordsman (as is quickly established in his defence of La Rappinière, p.71, and developed in the retrospective narrative, e.g. p.158), and an infallible defender of threatened female honour. His comportment is contrasted with the more risible of his companions, and rapidly contributes to his status as 'la figura

esemplare dell'attore-*honnête homme*' ('the exemplary figure of the
actor and *honnête homme*', *40*, p.5). Despite his humble origins, Le
Destin has clearly become a *de facto* noble both by inclination and
contamination. (Indeed, in Serroy's interpretation at least, Le Destin
was destined to be revealed as a nobleman in the third book, *5*,
p.341. Such a development can only have the status of a hypothesis,
however, and it still seems quite plausible within the confines of the
extant novel simply to see him as the beneficiary of his upbringing,
and thus as a triumph of nurture over nature.) He is furthermore a
man of action not of words, as we see in the Bouvillon seduction
chapter (II, x): 'Il ne savait que lui dire, outre qu'il parlait peu de son
naturel' (p.255). At the same time, even he has a caricatural quality,
albeit a sympathetically drawn one, most amusingly in his repeatedly
declared intention to seek death on the battlefield if disappointed in
love; and even he has an accident more redolent of Ragotin at the
comic climax to the Bouvillon episode (pp.257-58).

It is particularly in II, viii, in conversation with the 'jeune
conseiller de Rennes', La Garouffière, that his *honnêteté* is stressed,
a quality combining politeness ánd wit, self-knowledge and
frankness, breadth of culture and social skilfulness. La Garouffière is
a figure whose associations (however spurious) are with questions of
aesthetics in all the episodes in which he is involved, and who seems
to have accorded himself the role of arbiter of good taste in this
chapter above all. He is versed in Parisian manners, whereby he
achieves the rank, as the narrator rather archly comments, 'non pas
de noblesse tout à fait, mais de non-bourgeoisie, si j'ose ainsi parler'
(p.248), even if he is comically self-centred: 'La Garouffière [...]
était attentivement occupé à parler de vers au Destin, et à lui donner
bonne opinion de son esprit' (p.250). It is with him, then, that Le
Destin converses 'fort spirituellement' in 'une des plus belles
conversations qui se soient jamais faites dans une hôtellerie du bas
Maine', and in which Le Destin in particular 'discourut comme un
homme fort éclairé et qui savait bien son monde' (p.251). It is
apparently only after Le Destin's disquisition on 'femmes d'esprit'
however, worthy of La Rochefoucauld and entirely in the spirit of the
salons, that La Garouffière is reluctantly brought to recognize in

another the quality on which he so prides himself: 'La Garouffière, qui était fort honnête homme et qui se connaissait bien en honnêtes gens, ne pouvait comprendre comment un comédien de campagne pouvait avoir une si parfaite connaissance de la véritable honnêteté' (pp.251-52). Elsewhere we find Le Destin interjecting perceptive remarks, for example on clothes and rank, which reinforce this status in the reader's perception: 'J'étais assez bien vêtu, comme il est nécessaire de l'être à ceux de qui la condition ne peut faire excuser un méchant habit' (p.168); or half concealing a maxim-like phrase or *sententia*: 'la plupart du monde ne considère les personnes que selon qu'elles leur sont utiles' (p.171).

A final note about the members of the troupe must concern their names. As Adam notes, 'la plupart des comédiens du xviie siècle adoptaient un nom de théâtre' but equally 'Le Destin, La Rancune, ou La Caverne ne donnent pas une idée juste des noms communément adoptés' (*1*, p.533 n. 8). Here again, therefore, Scarron is taking a contemporary theatrical feature, but adding to it the elements of imagination and caricature which typify his character portrayal. Le Destin and L'Etoile form appropriately enough the couple of lovers brought together by the designs of fate; the name of Angélique is equally uncomplicated in its evocation of her beauty; La Rancune's name onomastically reflects his dominant temperament; and La Caverne exudes an unfathomable gloom. Only the (underdeveloped) L'Olive remains obscure, although an explanation would perhaps have been forthcoming in a later book (for example the attribution of his name to his skin colour or corpulence).

Alongside the atmosphere of the troupe, we glean a multiplicity of minor insights into the circumstances of the acting profession and into the technicalities of theatrical practice and stagecraft in the period. We quickly learn that the duration of a troupe's stay in a town is typically four or five days (p.68); that patronage is vital (that of La Rappinière is quickly secured, p.71); and that poverty is nonetheless rife (as we see from the old clothes having to be patched up, p.76). In I, v ('Qui ne contient pas grand-chose') a rapid résumé is afforded of the history of La Rancune, who is the unsuccessful actor *par excellence*, playing all the minor roles, whether they suited him or not: 'il jouait en fausset et, sous les masques, les rôles de nourrice' as well as 'de confidents, ambassadeurs et recors, quand il fallait accompagner un roi, prendre ou assassiner quelqu'un, ou donner bataille'. Furthermore, 'il chantait une méchante taille aux trios [...] et se farinait à la farce' (p.74). (Thus for Mariani, Le Destin is the 'attore nuovo' ['actor of the new generation'], La Rancune the 'attore della vecchia guardia' ['actor of the old school'], *40*, p.35.)

The first systematic exposition of the troupe and its constitution is reserved for the opening of I, viii ('Dans lequel on verra plusieurs choses nécessaires à savoir pour l'intelligence du présent livre'), and reveals the existence of the aspirant actor-valets alongside the three male principals, together with the contrasting roles typically taken by the younger and older actresses (with La Caverne, apart from farce, consigned to 'les reines et les mères'). In this context too we are given a further reminder of the difficulties of the career: 'c'est une des grandes incommodités du métier, laquelle, jointe à celle d'être obligé de pleurer et de rire lorsqu'on a envie de faire toute autre chose, diminue beaucoup le plaisir qu'ont les comédiens d'être quelquefois empereurs et impératrices, et être appelés beaux comme le jour, [...] bien qu'ils aient vieilli sur le théâtre et que leur cheveux et leurs dents fassent une partie de leurs hardes' (p.85). This underlying presence of disillusionment and fatigue adds to the feeling that we are given of being backstage rather than in the auditorium, always seeing the actors as such, before they become the characters they are playing. As Coulet remarks, 'l'image est gaie et poétique, mais elle est vraie, ni les misères ni les laideurs ne sont dissimulées' (*20*, p.205).

It is then again, and more importantly, through La Caverne that life in the theatrical family is described (II, iii). This brief biography of a 'comédienne née d'un comédien' gives a succinct sketch of the less glamorous side of the existence with its poverty and its uncertainties. She is born backstage, and her youth is based around the troupe in which she grows up, to discover the truth of the punning statement that 'la vie comique n'est pas si heureuse qu'elle le paraît' (p.220) – although it is noteworthy that travelling players are accorded a greater status of respectability than the 'bohémiens' in mistake for whom they are briefly captured in this chapter, just as they are differentiated from 'les paysans' in II, xvi. The theatre is indeed presented in one view at least as a 'métier' which, despite the fact that it is the churlish La Rancune who points to the fact (p.75), it is clearly not given to everyone to acquire, as the failed career of Ragotin, '[qui] n'était pas encore reçu dans l'ordre vagabond des comédiens de campagne' (p.304), will most signally illustrate. Reference is made elsewhere to the acme of contemporary ambition, and the troupe's actresses' misfortune in not reaching it: 'par malheur plutôt que faute de mérite elles [n'avaient] jamais eu l'honneur de monter sur le théâtre de l'hôtel de Bourgogne ou du Marais, qui sont et l'un et l'autre le *non plus ultra* des comédiens' (p.112). Even so, after a particularly successful performance late in the first part (taking place 'après dîner', that is in the late afternoon, following a morning rehearsal) of an unspecified play, we are told that 'ceux de l'assistance qui avaient souvent ouï la comédie dans Paris avouèrent que les comédiens du roi n'eussent pas mieux représenté' (p.164). Nonetheless a fundamental difference is underlined between Paris and the provinces, and we may understand that the troupe may still only aspire to the higher ideals of the Parisian theatre, where 'la comédie [...] est aujourd'hui purgée [...] de tout ce qu'elle avait de licencieux', and where the Hôtel de Bourgogne is scandalized by 'des équivoques basses et sales' (p.249). Relatedly, the narrator defends the morality of actresses; and indeed the actresses of the novel are all portrayed as reasonably honest, faithful and furthermore intelligent: 'les comédiennes, outre qu'elles étaient fort belles, étaient capables de dire autre chose que des vers appris par cœur' (p.184), a defence supported empirically by I, viii, in which Angélique ('très honnête fille') and L'Etoile are shown, in contrasting ways, as eminently capable of dealing with the surfeit of unwelcome advances to which they are subjected (p.85).

In the same chapter (II, iii), in which mobility is again a recurrent feature (and further picturesque convoys are described), the question of patronage is also developed, and the co-existence of freedom and dependence thus depicted. Details of the troupe's patrons occur at intervals, and late in the first book we learn: 'Ce jour-là les comédiens avaient été retenus pour représenter une comédie chez un des plus riches bourgeois de la ville, qui faisait un grand festin et donnait le bal aux noces d'une demoiselle de ses parentes dont il était tuteur' (p.180). We then read of the theatre being set up in preparation for the play, and note that the actors were well received, given changing rooms and meals, and allowed ample time to prepare for their performance. Clearly, the taste of the audiences dictates to a great extent the possibilities of production ('l'attore dà al pubblico quello che il pubblico desidera' ['the actor gives the audience what the audience wants'], *40*, p.69), but by the same token some obligation of hospitality clearly falls on the sponsor: 'Le baron [de Sigognac] nous faisait manger à sa table, ses gens nous servaient avec empressement et nous disaient souvent qu'ils nous étaient obligés de la bonne humeur de leur maître, qu'ils trouvaient tout changé depuis que la comédie l'avait humanisé' (p.225). The implicitly therapeutic effects of comedy are underlined in such a statement, as they will again be in Molière's *Le Malade imaginaire* (1673), and indeed, as we have seen, the defence of the theatre is an important topic throughout. A further new patron, the marquis d'Orsé, then makes his appearance upon the return of the troupe to Le Mans in II, xvii, inaugurating a festive period of plays, hunts and balls: 'Il aimait passionnément la comédie et tous ceux qui s'en mêlaient et c'est ce qui attirait tous les ans dans la capitale du Maine les meilleures troupes de comédiens du royaume' (p.312).

The theatrical nature of the primary subject matter is further reinforced by the overlap between the theatricality of the stage and the theatricality of the world, as underlined in the off-stage appearance of the troupe. As Rousset remarks (of the baroque aesthetic), 'le théâtre déborde hors du théâtre, envahit le monde [...], l'assujettit à ses propres lois de mobilité et de métamorphose' (*31*, p.28). Or, for Serroy, the theatre is a 'trait d'union entre le monde réel et l'univers de l'illusion, [et] fournit au romancier le thème idéal pour traduire cette dualité qui constitue le fond de son œuvre' (*5*, p.25). They are straightaway identified as visually striking, given Le Destin's costume and the improbable configuration of the shabby procession which is making its way into 'les halles du Mans'. And, as La Rappinière is quick to note, 'La Caverne, en son habit d'ordinaire, pourrait passer pour tout ce que l'on voudrait en une comédie' (p.68). Further parallels occur between the theatre and the world beyond the stage when, in I, v, 'La Rappinière reçut son [La Rancune's] compliment avec un faste de prévôt provincial et ne lui rendit pas la dixième partie des civilités qu'il en reçut; mais, comme les comédiens jouent toutes sortes de personnages, il ne s'en émut guère' (p.75). Le Destin uses an acting metaphor in the course of his story, claiming that 'je faisais auprès de sa mère mon vrai personnage, c'est-à-dire le paysan' (p.126); and even passages with no explicit theatrical subject-matter, such as the fight in I, xii, are curiously similar to a stage fight in their symmetry, rhythm and spectatorial response: 'Le Destin, s'étant acharné sur une grosse servante qu'il avait troussée, lui donna plus de cent claques sur les fesses. L'Olive, qui vit que cela faisait rire la compagnie, en fit autant à une autre' (p.115). Finally, L'Etoile is able to put her acting talent to good practical use after her abduction: 'Mademoiselle de L'Etoile fit encore mieux la malade à la chandelle qu'elle ne l'avait fait dans l'obscurité' (p.266).

In all these ways, Scarron both shows us the *grandeurs et misères* of the profession, but also, by virtue of the narrator's obvious and sometimes explicit sympathy for the prevalent ethos of it, contributes to and indeed creates the warmth of tone which characterizes the novel as a whole. Rousset writes in terms of '[une] contre-épopée des comédiens de campagne' (*44*, p.147); and, in a felicitous synthesis, Bénac evokes 'la troupe comique où chaque personnage, si irréel qu'il soit d'ailleurs, joue un rôle réel qui justement lui donne la vie et assure au *Roman comique* sa valeur d'un document dans l'histoire du théâtre français' (*2*, p.43).

3. *Comedy: the* burlesque

If we now turn from the theatrical to the comic element of the title, we must begin by attempting a definition of the *burlesque*, arguably the most widely approved and certainly the least anachronistic of all the possible definitions of the novel's character: 'Si le *Roman comique* est par certains de ses aspects une œuvre romanesque, il offre un autre caractère encore, qui achève de le définir. Il est un roman "divertissant". Il veut, de propos délibéré, nous faire rire [...] par les procédés du burlesque' (*1*, p.39). The primary definition of *burlesque* in terms of poetry would in fact apply more closely to Scarron's *Virgile travesti* than to the *Roman comique*; it is closely associated with parody and travesty, and describes either the transposition of an epic or heroic genre into comedy by means of the deliberate introduction of vulgarity and banality, or the deployment of elevated style in the account of the mundane. Although this parodic dimension will play an important role in the novel, however, it cannot account for the whole comic impact of the work. What we have also to bear in mind therefore is the broader sense of *burlesque*, perhaps as broad as that of *Le Robert*: 'qui est d'un comique outré, extravagant'. *Le Robert* also gives Faguet's definition: 'tantôt un jeu de l'imagination bouffe, tantôt un goût de reproduire avec exactitude les choses triviales'; and, most helpfully of all, provides the antonyms: *burlesque* is all that is *not* 'dramatique, grave, sérieux, tragique, triste, correct [ou] mesuré'. Etymologically, too, we find on the one hand the derivation of the term indicating no more than the idea of a joke (Italian 'burla'); and yet, as Cronk has shown, the French understanding in the earlier seventeenth century was predominantly linguistic: 'il semblera peut-être plus exact de parler du burlesque non pas comme un genre mais plutôt comme un style, comme une modalité d'écrire' (*21*, p.322).

Lack of seriousness, exaggeration, and parody thus all seem to be involved, and the *Roman comique* might indeed be felt to fall between a broad (modern) and a narrow (contemporary) definition of the term. It is undeniably in many of its episodes grotesque and exaggerated; but it also contains more sophisticated parody, if not of a single work, at least of the kinds of writing which collectively typify the novel in the period of its composition and before, most of which would in their original form have been devoid of any comic element, and would have been concerned with the activities of literary creations of a higher degree of moral and social nobility than travelling players. Added to this are all kinds of more local linguistic play: euphemism, bathos, pseudo-erudition, false logic, pun, zeugma, all accompanied by an acute degree of stylistic self-consciousness, and with the narrator frequently using metafictional intervention to draw attention to his own techniques.

If we concentrate initially on the broad comedy, we find that the term 'farcical' is also applicable, since there are several features in common with the characteristic devices of stage farce. In particular, we note the *topoi* (or commonplaces) of false or feigned death; of beatings, strenuously urged by the appropriately named père Giflot, who, 'quoique essouflé d'avoir couru, ne se lassait pas de crier: "Fouettez, fouettez!" de toute sa force; et le cocher de toute la sienne redoublait ses coups sur Ragotin' (p.310); and, most frequently of all, the theme of mistaken identity, usually under the cover of darkness. Indeed it is curious to note how many of the novel's chapters concern events which happen during the evening (particularly story-telling, eating and drinking) and, more frequently still, at night. This is partly no doubt for comic effect, in scenes whose sparking-off point is a non-recognition because of darkness (comparable in the theatrical domain to Act III of Molière's *George Dandin* (1668), for example), but also because, quite simply, sleeping together seems to have been as much a practical and communal activity as a sexual one, giving rise thereby to all sorts of escapades and discussions set in the bedroom. The first sequence of comic chapters of Part II takes place entirely at night; while the opening of II, viii offers a brief hiatus as Ragotin sleeps: 'Le reste du

jour se passa assez pacifiquement dans l'hôtellerie' (p.247), only to
return to activity as night falls (p.248). Indeed there is a contrast
established between the nocturnal escapades and narrations of the
troupe's members and its adjuncts (especially the comic ones) and
the ordinary business of the inn, which starts with daybreak: 'On se
leva de bonne heure, comme on fait toujours dans les hôtelleries où
le bruit commence avec le jour' (p.253).

Above all, we note the farcical use of comic sequences,
redolent of the *lazzi* (or routines) of the Italian *commedia dell'arte*
tradition. In the brilliantly scatological chapter concerning La
Rancune and his chamber-pot (I, vi), three repeated, but
progressively more frenetic actions lead to the 'copieuse éjaculation
d'urine' and its aftermath (pp.78-80). Again in II, xvii, in the course
of a quarrel between Ragotin and La Baguenodière, a threefold
dispute is explicitly resumed: '[La] Baguenodière tourna la tête pour
la troisième fois, pour la troisième fois regarda son homme et, pour
la troisième fois, se retourna vers le théâtre' (p.314). Similarly
related to farce rhythms by the deployment of a sequence is the
repeated refrain 'Je ne dis pas cela' of Madame Bouvillon in her
seduction scene with Le Destin, anticipating Molière's Alceste (*Le
Misanthrope* (1666), I, ii) both in phraseology and in intention.
Indeed the whole scene is highly theatrical, playing on the visually
comic qualities of La Bouvillon and their contrast with Le Destin's
modesty, and moving as it does to a comic Ragotin-*ex machina*
dénouement.

Elements of outright sexual obscenity are however non-
existent (in striking contrast to *Francion*); but at the same time there
are several further passages and episodes where a tone of *gauloiserie*
is established, where scatology or gluttony loom large, and where
Rabelais figures as a clear precursor. In II, viii, for example, a tone of
undisguised coarseness is struck:

> ...la jeune mariée trouva si plaisant que, s'ébouffant de
> rire en commençant de boire, elle couvrit le visage de sa
> belle-mère et celui de son mari de la plus grande partie

de ce qui était dans son verre et distribua le reste sur la
table et sur les habits de ceux qui y étaient assis. (p.250)

Yet even here the outcome of the episode is that everybody ends up
laughing, so that such a passage fits easily into the spirit of 'bonne
chère' and the general good humour of the work, evident too in the
description of a festive meal in II, xvi. Drinking, as in Rabelais, leads
to drunkenness, and there is a protracted episode at the end of II, xi
whose comedy depends on the drunken valets of Saldagne, by virtue
of whose inebriation the escape of L'Etoile is assured; I, xi depends
for its comic momentum on the progressive intoxication of La
Rancune and Ragotin; and one further chapter in the second part is
largely devoted to the drunkenness of Ragotin as a comic motif (II,
xvi).

    Two further elements of the *burlesque* which are much closer
to a tradition of farce than of parody are the inclusion of caricatures,
and the depiction of sustained scenes of disorder. Characterizations
of the more minor members of the troupe and their companions are
often brief and superficial, and progressively move towards
caricature as participants are relatively less extensively exploited
(and L'Olive never really attains a distinct characterization beyond
that of straight man in episodes with La Rancune). We are told that
the poet Roquebrune was, 'en son espèce, [...] aussi sot et aussi vain
que Ragotin' (p.163). He breaks immediately into name-dropping
and pretentiousness at the first opportunity; and, even though the
reader may forget his salient characteristics, the narrator does not.
Thus after a long period of neglect, Roquebrune's affectations are
ironically recalled in II, xiii, as the relatively recent figure of Inézille
begins her story, composed or translated 'à l'aide du divin
Roquebrune, qui lui avait juré par Apollon et les neuf Sœurs qu'il lui
apprendrait dans six mois toutes les grâces et les finesses de notre
langue' (p.319). One memorable pair of comic-strip portraits is that
of the 'hôte' and 'hôtesse' of II, vi. He is encapsulated by his
'cheveux de drille, plus longs que ceux des autres paysans du village,
ses serments à la soldate, une plume hérissée qu'il mettait les fêtes
quand il ne pleuvait point et une épée rouillée qui lui battait de

vieilles bottes encore qu'il n'eût point de cheval'; she more
succinctly: 'Le visage de cette nymphe tavernière était le plus petit et
son ventre était le plus grand du Maine, quoique cette province
abonde en personnes ventrues' (p.236). Their status as a grotesque
couple is further clinched by the death of the 'hôte', since
'[l'hôtesse] eut le plaisir de le voir mourir la tête cassée; ce qu'elle
attribuait à un juste jugement de Dieu, parce qu'il avait souvent joué
à casser la sienne' (p.236). The most memorable of all the cameo
figures is undoubtedly Madame Bouvillon, 'la grosse sensuelle', who
arrives on the scene as late as II, viii, but is the subject of a brilliant
extended portrait, affording the only intrusion in the text of
'aggressive, unvarnished sensuality' (*45*, p.133). The attempted
seduction of Le Destin by gluttony (p.250), followed by a more direct
assault (pp.256-57) are of a disconcerting perceptiveness, and
unashamed in their Fellini-esque exploitation of obesity and rampant
sensuality. In the second appearance, too, the visual component is
strong, the details of clothing of the 'petite nymphe replète' are
especially accurately described, and the caricatural status of the
whole is assured by the repeated use of hyperbole.

Such an impression is further enhanced by the use of comically
descriptive naming (in addition to the stage names of the troupe
members). Thus Ragotin's name clearly recalls the adjective 'ragot'
(small in stature and stocky), La Rappinière evokes 'la rapine'
(plunder), La Baguenodière's name resembles the verb
'baguenauder' (to waste time on trifles), 'bouvillon' means a young
bullock, and le père Giflot is immediately involved in beatings
('gifler', to slap); whereas names such as Sigognac and La
Garouffière are redolent of their provincial origins (in the latter case
accompanied by an explicit lesson in regional etymologies, p.248).
Furthermore basic descriptive epithets (such as 'le petit homme' for
Ragotin) and traits of behaviour tend to consistency. On the other
hand, in the cases of Ragotin, Roquebrune and, later and most
strikingly, La Garouffière, the names are introduced after the
characters, seeming to suggest that types are more important than
individuals, a view which would indeed be supported by the
emphases of the novel as a whole. We also find finely wrought

portraits, which the introductory description of La Rancune illustrates as well as any, finishing as it does with a typical contradiction after an unflattering enumeration: 'avec tout cela, le meilleur homme du monde' (pp.74-75). Such features are entirely in keeping with the work's central focus (the troupe), and lead me to disagree with critics such as Bénac (*2*, pp.62-71, *passim*) who implicitly regret the absence of a more naturalistic series of psychologies (and indeed 'psychologies' seems itself an inappropriate term). The potential afforded by interactions, comic routines and relative predictability is the business of the *Roman comique*, not subtle character portrayal or development; and the same is as (or more) true of the more marginal figures (and, *a fortiori*, of the supporting figures of the interpolated or retrospective narrations). Much later in the first book, therefore, the listeners' reactions to the promise of a Spanish *nouvelle* narrated by Inézille fall entirely within the caricatures which are by now well established (p.186).

The greatest comic talent of Scarron lies however in his ability to assemble and sustain scenes of physical disorder over long periods of narrative, and to bring clarity to chaos in so doing. The *Roman comique* abounds in episodes involving an exponential spread of confusion, usually beginning with two or three participants before developing into a free-for-all, and invariably characterized by physical violence. We especially note the use of comic crescendo, most powerfully illustrated in II, xvi, as a sequence of humiliations pursues the unfortunate Ragotin, to be resumed in the synthetic closing cadence of the chapter, where the satisfaction of his return to Le Mans 'lui fit oublier la chute de la charrette, les coups de fouet du cocher, les morsures du chien et les piqûres des mouches' (p.311). The *Roman comique* is an extraordinarily physical, not to say violent book: fights are more or less daily occurrences, as are accidents, abductions and even deaths – that, for example, of the 'hôte' (II, vi) being treated without an ounce of sentimentality, and indeed with a good deal of awareness of its comic potential. (The fragility of life is an omnipresent, if inexplicit, theme.) In this context we might single out in particular I, xii, xiv, xv, xvii; II, vi, vii; and above all II, xvii, a passage where there are two related episodes going on at the same

time, described by the narrator himself as 'ce hideux chaos'. The
scene proposes in addition a disparity between comic cause and
effect, succinctly pointed by the narrator's aside ('Jamais un aussi
petit sujet ne causa de plus grands accidents', p.315); yet within the
general turmoil, there is always a degree of clarity, just as there
would be in a highly-coloured and complex painting[3]. Scarron is
careful in this episode, for example, to repeat names, so that readers
can follow what is going on, even if they lack a complete mental
picture; and sentences (or their component parts) are systematically
kept short, so that an effect of rapidity of incident and breathlessness
is achieved. Bénac notes how 'Scarron élargit son comique à des
visions d'ensemble, à de véritables fresques' (*2*, p.60); yet at the
same time they are not disproportionate within the overall economy
of the work as a whole. Furthermore, they depend precisely on
cumulative disorder for their effect, as well as being complete and
self-contained within themselves.

     The visual dimension to such scenes is indeed primary, with
just enough pertinent details sketched in to fix an image in the
reader's mind without an exhaustive proto-balzacian accumulation;
and the idea of the sketch, 'l'art du croquis rapide' (*2*, p.56), is often
apposite in describing many of Scarron's most brilliant scenes,
characterized as they are by the avoidance of heaviness or tedium.
We notice this for example in I, xiv, where a tableau is quickly
afforded of the stretcher-bearing party. The contrast between the
imperviously sleeping curé and the terror endured by his niece and
valets shows the sinister being turned into broad farce, with the
different reactions caricaturally encapsulated in a single phrase, and
the whole picture alive with colour and detail: 'La nièce du curé était
plus morte que vive; Guillaume et Julian pleuraient sans oser ouvrir

---

[3] Indeed the novel was recurrently the subject of illustrations (see *41*). The most
celebrated engravings, by J.-B. Oudry (1686-1755), the *Recueil de 26 sujets
grotesques, représentant les plus intéressants passages de la vie de Ragotin tirés du
Roman comique de Scarron* (Paris, circa 1730) are reproduced in the 1892 edition of
the Tom Brown translation (see Appendix I and *46*). And the charmingly urbane
interpretations of Le Barbier enliven the three-volume edition of 'L'An quatrième'
(September 1795 - August 1796).

la bouche, à cause de l'effroyable vision des armes à feu; et le curé
dormait toujours, comme je vous ai déjà dit'. Even the horse is
accorded the status of an actor in the drama, as the choice of motives
so characteristic of the novel as a whole is extended to its stumbling,
'ou par belle malice, ou parce que l'on le faisait aller plus vite qu'il
ne lui était permis par sa nature pesante et endormie' (p.134). I, xvii
also begins with a striking visual sequence, which extracts cannot
easily convey. Ragotin, in attempting to be gallant, takes the hands of
the (much taller) La Caverne and Angélique as they return from the
performance of a play. The narrator takes over:

> Cette double civilité fut cause d'une incommodité triple;
> car La Caverne, qui avait le haut de la rue, comme de
> raison, était pressée par Ragotin, afin qu'Angélique ne
> marchât point dans le ruisseau. De plus, le petit homme,
> qui ne leur venait qu'à la ceinture, tirait si fort leurs
> mains en bas qu'elles avaient bien de la peine à
> s'empêcher de tomber sur lui. Ce qui les incommodait
> encore davantage, c'est qu'il se retournait à tout moment
> pour regarder mademoiselle de L'Etoile, qu'il entendait
> parler derrière lui à deux godelureaux qui la remenaient
> malgré elle. (p.165)

The idea is conventional, physical and unsophisticated. Yet here
again it is used with economy in a simple amplification (as they try
to cross on a staircase a valet carrying a bag of oats) and over
sufficiently brief a period to allow it the maximum comic
development within the artistic balance of the whole. The description
in the final chapter (II, xx) of Ragotin dozing is exceptionally
efficient and accurate, even managing to finish on a barbed simile: 'Il
ne dormait donc pas de toute sa force, laissant souvent aller sa tête
jusqu'à ses genoux et la relevant tantôt demi-endormi, et tantôt se
réveillant en sursaut, comme on fait plus souvent qu'ailleurs au
sermon quand on s'y ennuie' (p.342). Other similes may also enliven
the reader's capacity for visualization, such as in describing how La
Rancune leans over his bedfellow, 'comme on fait quand on veut

amasser quelque chose qui est à terre' (p.79); and visual *rappels* are also provided from chapter to chapter so that, in the course of a comic succession (such as II, vi-vii), certain striking details are briefly recalled from a previous episode.

The various processions, more often than not incongruous in their composition, are especially memorable, from that which opens the very first chapter throughout the whole novel. Typical of these would be the episode recalled in Le Destin's narration, predicted by the remark: 'Nous arrivâmes à Orléans, où notre entrée fut si plaisante que je vous en veux apprendre les particularités', and then introduced as follows:

> Nous entrâmes dans la ville dans l'ordre que je vais vous dire. Huit grands pendards ivres, ou qui le devaient être, portaient au milieu d'eux une petite cassette, comme je vous ai déjà dit. Mes pistolets suivaient l'un après l'autre, chacun porté par deux hommes. Mademoiselle de La Boissière, qui enrageait aussi bien que moi, allait immédiatement après: elle était assise dans une grande chaise de paille soutenue sur deux grands bâtons de batelier et portée par quatre hommes qui se relayaient les uns les autres et qui lui disaient cent sottises en la portant. (p.172)

More improbable details ensue, and the whole episode is reflected in the reaction of the townsfolk, whose curiosity underscores the *pittoresque* of the event: 'Durant notre marche, les passants s'arrêtaient dans les rues pour nous considérer et le bruit que l'on y faisait à cause de nous attirait tout le monde aux fenêtres' (p.173).

As we see in this and similar passages, the visual impression is matched by the element of noise. There can be few more rowdy novels than the *Roman comique* and, even in a more domestic setting, we often explicitly or implicitly understand that 'chacun parlait de toute sa force sans entendre ce que disaient les autres' (p.103); indeed the episode in the 'histoire de La Caverne' (II, iii) of her family's troupe's capture approaches its resolution when 'le bruit que nous faisions et que faisaient les brutaux et les ivrognes qui nous avaient amenés fit sortir d'une salle basse le seigneur du château' (p.221). Similarly, the 'hôtesse' reacts to her husband's death by wailing ostentatiously (p.237), an activity in which she is then joined in the following chapter: 'En achevant de parler, elle se mit à hurler; et les autres femmes, comme de concert, lui répondirent en chœur et toutes ensemble firent un bruit si grand et si lamentable que tout ce qu'il y avait de gens dans l'hôtellerie entra dans la chambre et ce qu'il y avait de voisins et de passants entra dans l'hôtellerie' (p.242). Shortly thereafter the curé appears briefly to try to restore order, but he is eventually defeated in his efforts by the din, so that 'le pauvre bonhomme fut contraint de se boucher les oreilles et de gagner la porte' (p.245).

If we next turn to those episodes where the two ideas of the *burlesque* overlap, we find in them the deployment of elevated language and euphemism in the treatment of coarse themes, so that 'la grossièreté est comme déchargée de toute inconvenance par la magie des mots' (*32*, p.513); and indeed the exploitation of instability of register is a vital feature of Scarron's narrative technique. We might single out the delightful passage in I, xv describing a pack of dogs following a bitch on heat in pseudo-anthropomorphic terms (and there are periodic shifts between anthropomorphism and zoomorphism), and who knock over a portable organ. This is both broad comedy and pure, parodic *burlesque* in the technical sense of the word. 'Ces amants immodérés', who are pursuing 'leur maîtresse', who is a 'chienne de mauvaise vie', have their characteristic behaviour described in a mixture of crude language on the one hand and elegant syntax and periphrasis on the other:

...ils renversèrent une table à tréteaux qui soutenait la machine harmonieuse et je ne voudrais pas jurer que quelques-uns de ces maudits chiens ne levassent la jambe et ne pissassent contre les orgues renversées, ces animaux étant fort diurétiques de leur nature, principalement quand quelque chienne de leur connaiss-

ance a envie de procéder à la multiplication de son
espèce. (pp.160-61)

Again, more simply, of Ragotin: 'son adversaire [...] le fit aller choir
sur le cul au pied des comédiennes après une rétrogradation fort
précipitée' (p.103). Finally, at the end of the chamber-pot episode,
'le pauvre marchand le [La Rancune] félicitait le mieux qu'il pouvait
de sa copieuse éjaculation d'urine qui lui faisait espérer un sommeil
qui ne serait plus interrompu' (p.79). This leads in turn to La
Rancune's splendidly dignified reaction as his victim is covered in
urine: '"Voilà un grand malheur!"' (p.80), with the instability of
register again manipulated to maximum contrastive, and thus comic,
effect.

     Turning finally to pure *burlesque*, we find it most strikingly
illustrated in the very first self-conscious paragraphs of the whole
work. Indeed the opening of the novel accurately sets the tone for
much that will follow, and the use of bathos rapidly confirms the
burlesque status:

     Le soleil avait achevé plus de la moitié de sa course et
     son char, ayant attrapé le penchant du monde, roulait
     plus vite qu'il ne voulait. Si ses chevaux eussent voulu
     profiter de la pente du chemin, ils eussent achevé ce qui
     restait du jour en moins d'un demi-quart d'heure; mais,
     au lieu de tirer de toute leur force, ils ne s'amusaient
     qu'à faire des courbettes, respirant un air marin qui les
     faisait hennir et les avertissait que la mer était proche, où
     l'on dit que leur maître se couche toutes les nuits. Pour
     parler plus humainement et plus intelligiblement, il était
     entre cinq et six quand une charrette entra dans les halles
     du Mans. (p.65)

Simon speaks here of a 'parody of the ornate style of the
conventional heroic novels, set against a more "human" way of
writing' (*45*, p.131); and indeed the juxtaposition of the 'char' of the
sun with the 'charrette' of the actors immediately contrasts the epic

with the down-to-earth. Another major example occurs in I, xx, where verbal comedy follows on immediately from visual comedy, via a narratorial intervention, so that two comic effects are drawn from the same episode, and the same kind of play between elevated language and its abandonment is proposed as in the novel's opening paragraph. After the maximum visual impact has been derived from Ragotin's equestrian incompetence, the narrator continues:

> Aussitôt que l'infortuné Ragotin ne se sentit qu'un pommeau de selle entre les deux parties de son corps qui étaient les plus charnues et sur lesquelles il avait accoutumé de s'asseoir, comme font tous les autres animaux raisonnables; je veux dire qu'aussitôt qu'il se sentît n'être assis que sur fort peu de chose [...] (pp.182-83)

The *burlesque* is underlined in both these examples, as the narrator draws attention to the elevated register by the simple device of abandoning it, a tendency that may also be more gradually deployed, while still giving ample scope for effects of bathos: the cadence of I, iii, for example, proceeds: 'Le bienfait trouva place en son cœur de roche; et, sans vouloir permettre que ces pauvres restes d'une troupe délabrée allassent loger en une hôtellerie, il les emmena chez lui où le charretier déchargea le bagage comique et s'en retourna à son village' (p.71).

Self-conscious periphrasis is used more simply, for example in II, xvi, when Ragotin is stung, as 'ces petits éléphants ailés, pourvu de proboscides et armés d'aiguillons, s'acharnèrent sur ce petit corps nu qui n'avait point de mains pour se défendre et le blessèrent d'une horrible manière', until 'le meunier retira Ragotin d'entre les glaives pointues et venimeux de ces ennemis volants' (pp.310-11). Elsewhere Roquebrune's backside is described as 'les parties de derrière du citoyen de Parnasse' (p.183 – perhaps his pseudo-poetic status makes him particularly susceptible to comic periphrasis, since he is elsewhere referred to as '[le] nourrisson des Muses', p.163). Certain brief high-register outbursts then interrrupt even (especially)

the most frenetic of narrations, thus in II, vii, at one point: 'La
Rancune et L'Olive s'étaient si peu étonnés, et de la terreur panique
de Ragotin, et de la transmigration d'un corps mort d'une chambre à
l'autre sans aucun secours humain, au moins dont on eût
connaissance, que [...]' (p.243); and, shortly thereafter, we learn via a
momentary return to the classical elevation of the opening
paragraphs, that 'la Discorde aux crins de couleuvre n'avait pas
encore fait dans cette maison-là tout ce qu'elle avait envie d'y faire'
(p.245). Euphemism occurs in the delightful: 'Ils furent ensemble le
reste du jour et se plurent tellement l'un à l'autre que la nuit même
ils en dormirent moins qu'ils n'avaient accoutumé' (p.188). Or
describing the death of the 'hôte' in II, vi: 'Pendant
l'accommodement, l'hôte acheva son obscure destinée sans en
avertir ses amis' (p.237). Yet more strained examples occur in the
interpolated stories, in accordance with their greater decorum, and
consonant with their higher social settings. As we read of the finally
reunited Dom Carlos and Porcia at the end of Ragotin's tale: 'On dit
qu'ils se levèrent bien tard le lendemain; ce que je n'ai pas grand-
peine à croire' (p.102). Literary terms are strikingly introduced in a
comic context, such as when the curé de Domfront shouts at his
niece, 'au nom de laquelle il joignait souvent l'épithète de double
carogne' (p.134), or the poet defends his 'hyperboles quotidiennes'
(p.164). Elsewhere, Scarron may indulge in a different form of the
same *burlesque* tendency, and employ elevated syntax rather than
lexis, such as when he brings a ternary structure into an otherwise
randomly organized passage: 'Le Destin, qui n'avait pas mangé de
tout le jour et avait fait beaucoup d'exercice, mangea très avidement.
Léandre se reput d'amoureuses pensées plus que de viandes et le curé
parla plus qu'il ne mangea' (p.237). This intermingling of
informative and relatively familiar language with self-consciously
elevated usage thus characterizes the work as a whole; instability of
register recurs at all points, both from chapter to chapter, but also
from paragraph to paragraph and even within smaller units of
writing. As Serroy remarks, 'maître du burlesque, [Scarron] sait
jouer des décalages et des ruptures' (*5*, p.29). In this way too, the
broader features of the text as a whole are reflected in its detail.

Other more minor incidents of parodic literary devices are
common throughout. Scarron's lexis is often picturesque, and is
shown to best advantage in his well-developed gift for the
appropriate metaphor or simile, such as in the (presumably) popular
expression: 'le malicieux comédien, qui était homme à s'éborgner
pour faire perdre un œil à un autre' (p.78). The simile may be
felicitously used to *pittoresque* effect: 'La Caverne et sa fille [...]
parurent à la porte de la chambre avec de la lumière, comme le feu
Saint-Elme après une tempête' (p.114); 'Il n'y avait pas longtemps
qu'il dormait, ronflant comme une pédale d'orgue' (p.306); or, more
extended: 'On eût pu comparer La Baguenodière à un grand dogue et
Ragotin à un roquet qui aboie après lui sans que le dogue en fasse
autre chose que d'aller pisser contre une muraille' (pp.314-15),
replacing the anthropomorphism of our earlier quotation by the
zoomorphic. Here too, as in many other areas of linguistic
exuberance, the narrator may draw attention to his own techniques,
such as the parenthetically defined occurrence of synecdoche:
'l'hôtesse reçut un coup de poing dans son petit œil qui lui fit voir
cent mille chandelles (c'est un nombre certain pour un incertain) et la
mit hors de combat' (p.244 – the self-consciousness is reinforced by
the narrator explaining one half of the metaphor and not the other).
An improbable simile is defended early on by a specific
qualification: 'Quelque critique murmurera de la comparaison
[between La Rancune and a tortoise], à cause du peu de proportion
qu'il y a d'une tortue à un homme; mais j'entends parler des grandes
tortues qui se trouvent dans les Indes' (p.66). Other variants on self-
consciousness, still with regard to the simile, are achieved by an
explanation being provided in a tacit parenthesis: 'l'ascendant qu'il
avait sur lui était si grand que je l'ose comparer à celui du génie
d'Auguste sur celui d'Antoine: cela s'entend prix pour prix et sans
faire comparaison de deux comédiens de campagne à deux Romains
de ce calibre-là' (p.164); by the terms being subjected to a value
judgement: 'Elle lui sauta aux yeux, furieuse comme une lionne à qui
on a ravi ses petits (j'ai peur que la comparaison ne soit ici trop
magnifique)' (p.243); or by the self-evident simile, such as when a
hostelry valet tips a sack of oats down a staircase, 'jurant comme un

valet d'hôtellerie' (p.166), or of a horse 'qui reculait toujours, ronflant, soufflant et bronchant comme un cheval effarouché qu'il était' (p.269). It is of course the sheer inventiveness of Scarron's similes elsewhere, as his frequent deployment of them with commentaries, that allows for the successful comic impact of such bathetic devices.

In addition, various forms of simpler word play abound, in the form of puns and zeugma. Puns are rapid and effective: 'L'un jurait, l'autre injuriait' (p.70); 'quoiqu'il fût bien soûl, [il] sentit bien qu'il était seul' (p.73); 'Le pot de chambre du curé [...] avait été écuré' (p.133); 'le concert étant ainsi déconcerté' (p.161); zeugma, where a single verb governs two or more nouns in contrasting functions, is of necessity rather more developed: 'La Rappinière, selon sa coutume, eut grande peur et pensa bien avoir quelque chose de pis' (p.71); or 'je reprenais mon siège, ma couronne et ma gravité' (p.68). As Cronk notes, 'la langue burlesque écarte le mot de la chose, mais pour mieux attirer notre attention sur le mot même' (*21*, p.328).

Turning in conclusion to other comic uses of language, we find a variety of stylistic devices adapted to comic purposes. Scarron deploys the comic coda, for example, such as at the end of the episode of Ragotin's incompetent horsemanship: 'Enfin le pied se décrocha, ses mains lâchèrent le crin et il fallut tomber; *ce qu'il fit bien plus adroitement qu'il n'avait monté*' (p.183, my emphasis). The comic use of paralipsis (the denial of what is about to be done or said) occurs in Le Destin's narrative: 'Je vous avoue que les sentiments de respect et d'amitié que l'on doit avoir pour un père n'empêchèrent point que je ne le regardasse comme un très fâcheux vieillard' (p.143). Elsewhere, we encounter a kind of absurd logic, again reminiscent of Rabelais, in the meanness of the 'hôte' as recounted by the curé in II, vi; or in the surreal justification of an improbable event in terms of the impossible: 'comme tout le monde sait, quatre brancards se peuvent plutôt rencontrer ensemble que quatre montagnes' (p.133). Finally, verbal wit may be transferred to a speaking actor, such as in the sardonic (if, as it transpires, inaccurate) words of La Rancune upon the same accumulation of stretchers: '"Je crois que tous les brancards de la province se sont ici donné rendez-vous pour une affaire d'importance ou pour un chapitre général [...], et je suis d'avis qu'ils commencent leur conférence, car il n'y a pas apparence qu'il y en arrive davantage"' (p.83). Or by means of characterization through dialogue, as for example in a stunningly vacuous conversation between La Rancune and Ragotin:

> [Ragotin] fit entendre à La Rancune qu'une des comédiennes lui plaisait infiniment. "Et laquelle?" lui dit La Rancune. Le petit homme était si troublé d'en avoir tant dit qu'il répondit: "Je ne sais. – Ni moi aussi", dit La Rancune. Cela le troubla encore davantage et lui fit ajouter tout interdit: "C'est... c'est..." Il répéta quatre ou cinq fois le même mot dont le comédien, s'impatientant, lui dit: "Vous avez raison; c'est une fort belle fille." Cela acheva de le défaire. (p.108)

If Scarron has a peculiar and unique comic language, we nonetheless find in his subject matter elements of familiar comic ground, shared with many of his contemporaries, in the jibes against the commonplace butts of comic writers and *moralistes*. When we read of his characters talking about such topics as the secretive man (Roquebrune) who has nothing to say (p.179), doctors (pp.133; 230; 253), the *bourgeois gentilhomme* (pp.180; 304), dull-witted servants (p.134) or the interplay of the humours (p.305), we are immediately reminded of Molière, Boileau*, or La Bruyère. His persona too, in common with other contemporary comic writers, defends his work in terms of a development of the *castigat ridendo mores* tag, according to which laughter would correct the worst excesses of behaviour whilst affording innocent pleasure in the process:

> Peut-être aussi que j'ai un dessein arrêté et que, sans emplir mon livre d'exemples à imiter, par des peintures d'actions et de choses tantôt ridicules, tantôt blâmables, j'instruirai en divertissant de la même façon qu'un ivrogne donne de l'aversion pour son vice et peut

> quelquefois donner du plaisir par les impertinences que
> lui fait faire son ivrognerie. (p.111)

We first of all note the prevalent ambiguity ('this is not what I am doing, this is what I might be doing') in phrases such as 'peut-être aussi que [...]' but also the classical coexistence of 'plaire et instruire' (see *27*). And yet the way in which the same passage ends: 'Finissons la moralité et reprenons nos comédiens que nous avons laissés dans l'hôtellerie' (p.111) lays the emphasis firmly on the pleasure of the enterprise over and against any putative corrective function.

The question of morals and decorum, in particular where religion is concerned, is therefore worth a brief mention. The degree of moral rectitude in the story is relatively high, but such themes as illegitimacy, petty theft and violent brawls do have a certain currency. Drunkenness (as opposed to general 'bonne chère') is commonplace, as we have seen, although reserved mostly for the sinister or caricatural figures: 'La Rappinière but tant qu'il s'enivra et La Rancune s'en donna aussi jusques aux gardes' (p.73 – Le Destin, by contrast, 'soupa fort sobrement en honnête homme'). The most sensitive area in a comic work must however concern the Church, since the relationship between it and the acting profession was growing increasingly conflictual in the period, and was to reach its nadir in the polemic surrounding Molière's *Tartuffe* (1664). The cameo figure of the curé de Domfront seems affable and decently worldly; and the curé of II, vi, too, is 'honnête homme et savait bien son monde' (p.236). He is later again praised as being an 'homme d'esprit [qui] avait grand crédit parmi ses paroissiens' (p.245), and is soon accorded the epithet 'le bon curé' by the narrator after Angélique has been found and, since the hostelry was full, 'lui fit donner une chambre chez sa sœur qui logeait dans la maison voisine et qui était veuve d'un des plus riches fermiers du pays' (p.259 – there are tempting but perhaps fortuitous Biblical parallels with the crowded inn, all the more so given that the excluded figure is called Angélique).

Jesuit teachers on the other hand are described in passing as 'de si malplaisants maîtres' (p.232); and *bien-pensant* prudes are roundly attacked by the narrator (in discussing the judgement on a story) as old women whose 'enjouement de leur jeunesse [a] été plus scandaleux que le chagrin de leurs rides n'a été de bon exemple' (p.323); but this is again a *topos*, whose impact is further weakened by his going on to explain that Spanish customs were in any case different from French ones. There is a passing joke about the office of *Tenebrae* (p.160); one interpolated incident concerns the use of church services for flirtation (p.192); and on one or two occasions a tone of gentle familiarity with religious language is introduced: thus of provincial *tripots*, 'chacun y est reçu pour railler selon le talent qu'il en a eu du Seigneur' (p.69); or, ironically, of the authority of La Rappinière: '[Ragotin] les [Bohémiens] menaça aussi du lieutenant de prévôt La Rappinière au nom duquel tout genou fléchissait' (p.304). A mildly scabrous (and visually exuberant) scene involves the abbesse d'Estival, five or six nuns, the convent's director (le père Giflot, 'à qui la colère avait fait oublier pour un temps la charité') and the naked figure of Ragotin (pp.309-11); but arguably the most daring idea concerns the comically literal understanding of resurrection held by the 'hôtesse': 'Elle lui [l'hôte] demanda enfin comment il pourrait paraître dans la vallée de Josaphat, un méchant drap tout troué sur les épaules, et en quel équipage il pensait ressusciter. Le malade s'en mit en colère et, jurant comme il avait accoutumé en sa santé: "Eh! morbleu, vilaine! s'écria-t-il, je ne veux point ressusciter"' (p.238). Finally, a mad priest appears in II, xvi, '[qui] voulut faire imprimer quelques pensées creuses qu'il avait eues sur l'Apocalypse' (p.308), although his function seems predominantly to allow a claim of veracity to be made by the author persona, with whom he shares a printer. Overall there is nothing that is more than mildly scandalous in this domain, and what Coulet concludes in the context of a discussion of I, vi could well be more broadly applied: 'Cette page de littérature comique, malgré la grossièreté du sujet, [se range] au niveau de la littérature noble par la perfection artistique et la vérité morale' (*20*, p.204).

Such an examination of the detail of Scarron's comic writing must in turn lead us to look at two broader features which combine as the guiding narrative characteristics of the work as a whole, and under which I shall group my remarks in the next chapters: the novel's structure, particularly with regard to the *récit cadre* and the *romanesque*; and the function of the author / author persona / narrator.

4. Structure (i): the récit cadre

The structural complexity and authorial / narratorial stance in the *Roman comique* have occupied a great deal of critical attention, combining as they do at all stages to disconcert the reader, who is repeatedly pulled between discerning a principle of control and organization, and its refutation in the claims of non-omniscience and negligence. It is therefore timely to consider the most crucial aspect of the question of randomness as against organization by looking at the narrative levels, which afford a mixture of continuity and contrast, of apparent carelessness and artifice, combining in an 'unusual and complex structure composed of intrusive commentaries and a polyphonic blend of different narrative voices' (*28*, p.104).

The primary narrative level of the novel, the *récit cadre*, is situated in the recent past relative to the moment of narration. It provides a structural framework, over a limited time-scale, in the form of a racy narrative of some degree of realism, described as 'ces très véritables et très peu héroïques aventures' (p.111). It contains in turn the *romanesque* and retrospective second levels (see chapter 5); and it is periodically glossed by metafictional interventions (see chapter 6). Despite the often frenetic accumulation of incident – the journeyings, the upheavals of the players, the Ragotin episodes – there is however very little forward progress, either spatially or temporally. Questions therefore remain as to whether this narrative level, which certainly does not have any clear sense of direction, is thus entirely random, or whether it offers a structure, despite the repeated claims to the contrary. Certainly the author persona is at pains to emphasize the freedom of his writing: ' [...] un chapitre attire l'autre et [...] je fais dans mon livre comme ceux qui mettent la bride sur le col de leurs chevaux et les laissent aller sur leur bonne foi' (p.111). And Coulet notes how Scarron, 'pour faire apparaître la gratuité de l'invention romanesque, [affecte] d'élaborer son œuvre sous les yeux du lecteur, sans savoir où il [va]' (*20*, p.274).

The *Roman comique* is divided into two unequal parts, and subdivided into chapters of varying, but broadly similar length. This use of chapters and in particular of chapter-headings to indicate in some detail their content is borrowed from the Spanish model furnished by Cervantes in *Don Quijote*; and in both cases there is in addition an element of self-deflation introduced into many of the headings, as a quick glance at those of the *Roman comique* will indicate. Some are no more than minimally descriptive, such as 'Le plus court du présent livre' (I, xx), whereas others give value judgements as to their interest: 'Des moins divertissants du présent volume' (II, xi). In the majority of cases some thematic clue is given as to what will ensue, although even here the balance between the chapter title and its contents may well be misrepresented (e.g. I, vi); and the chapter entitled 'Ce qui arriva au pied de Ragotin' (II, viii) in fact only deals very cursorily with this business before going on to develop the contrastively important roles of La Garouffière and Madame Bouvillon, and to incorporate the apologia for the contemporary theatre.

There is some further symmetry provided by the openings and closings of the two volumes. Both parts of the novel begin with a parody-epic evocation of the time of day (the first evening, the second, more briefly, night), but the overall time-scale is so shifting as to give these opening passages little more than a set-piece quality; they afford no dynamic to the narrative, and they are each followed by an unrelated event: the arrival of the actors in Le Mans; and the further adventures of Le Destin. The second part opens as well with a strong sense of a new start, although narrative links are quickly established and *rappels* provided, notably of the function and potential of Ragotin (pp.218-19).

If we turn to the endings of both parts, we see how, just like the openings, there is some superficial similarity. The pattern which makes some sense of them concerns the *raison d'être* of the players, namely the performance of a play. Yet the first part ends on a non-performance: 'Malheur imprévu qui fut cause qu'on ne joua point la comédie', and as such appears very likely to be a deliberate anti-climax. It points too in a self-conscious way to the arbitrary functioning of the basic narrative level: that is, that although it provides a convenient chronological framework, it does not in fact narrate, in the first part at least, what it might be expected to. (And, here again, we might feel we are moving towards the idea of an anti-novel.) The first part ends rather on three features which in a minor form encapsulate the text's characteristics as a whole: the promise of a suggested 'Histoire d'Angélique et de Léandre' to come (so a further retrospective narrative); a sense of incompleteness in the primary narrative, with nothing more than a hiatus in the activity of the protagonists; and finally a trite *sententia* from the narrator to bring the book to a fragile close: 'Roquebrune, qui n'osa honnêtement quitter les comédiennes, en fut bien fâché, mais on n'a pas en ce monde tout ce qu'on désire' (p.208). The second part ends less symmetrically, since two chapters, one a quite long interpolated Spanish story, and the second a short Ragotin episode, follow what one might have thought to be the counterpoint to the end of the first part, namely the performance of plays by the actors without interruption: 'On représenta le jour suivant le *Nicomède* de l'inimitable monsieur de Corneille [...]. La représentation n'en fut point troublée et ce fut peut-être à cause que Ragotin ne s'y trouva pas' (p.317). It could then be argued that the second part would more convincingly have ended here, except that if we once again make a comparison with the first, we find that here too there is an interpolated chapter immediately preceding the conclusion. Or perhaps the last two chapters are added as a deliberate unbalancer – certainly the final chapter has a particularly inconclusive tone (in ironic distinction to various non-final chapters).

In either case, the perpetual tension between structuring and randomness becomes at once a characteristic and an endearing feature of the work, and the sense of care being taken to create carelessness, that *ars est celare artem*, is a recurrent one. The points at which the beginnings and endings of the volumes occur may apparently be random (and this is as true of the impression created by the opening of the whole work as of the subsequent divisions), yet there seems in fact to be some attention given to the formal composition of the exposition and dénouement(s). Giraud's evocation of 'une disposition symétrique souple' (*4*, p.25) is perhaps the most helpful summary[4].

There exist as well certain curious links within the overall structure. Although incident follows incident, often of the most fortuitous kind (attacks, accidents, brawls, delays and so on), and although new characters are introduced at all stages of the work, nevertheless some of these apparently random details are in fact recalled. Perhaps the most obvious development of this kind is the 'brancard' story (I, vii). During this chapter, as a stretcher-party takes off to fetch L'Etoile, and they stop for refreshment (a typical kind of delaying tactic), no fewer than three other parties carrying stretchers also arrive, one of which is carrying the curé de Domfront, 'qui [...] passait au Mans pour faire faire une consultation de médecins sur sa maladie' (p.83). This incident is then forgotten about entirely until, apparently quite at random, a story about the abduction of the curé is told, stemming from the previous incident (I, xiv). Again in 'Des bottes' (II, ii), La Rancune steals the boots of a fellow guest at a hostelry, which are then passed on to Ragotin, a fact that the reader is expected to remember when there is an explicit reference made back to it (II, xvi, p.306 – is this perhaps the reason for the earlier chapter title?); and shortly thereafter a passing madman from the first chapter of the second part makes an equally cursory reappearance in order to rob the already humiliated Ragotin of his belongings. The appearance of Le Destin and his companions at the novel's opening is explicitly recalled in I, xii as 'l'équipage que l'on a pu voir au début dans le commencement de ces très véritables et très peu héroïques aventures' (p.111); and as late as II, xv, the same episode is evoked (together with a further definition of the text): 'comme l'on a pu voir au

---

[4] To which we might add a useful if somewhat wordy definition afforded by Orr of the 'nonaristotelian novel': 'it is nonmimetic and calls our attention to its fictive nature; it is nonchronological but not achronological, since it foregrounds time or draws attention to the way in which our orderly expectations of time conventions in fiction are disarranged; and nonteleological, since the privileged position of the ending occurs only with chronological or logical narration' (*29*, p.31).

commencement de ces aventures comiques' (p.301). In addition, a series of more or less explicit *rappels* guides the implied reader in his bumpy passage through the story, thus: 'comme l'on a pu voir dans le septième chapitre' (p.113); or: 'Ceux qui auront eu assez de temps à perdre pour l'avoir employé à lire les chapitres précédents doivent savoir, s'il ne l'ont oublié, que le curé de Domfront était dans l'un des brancards qui se trouvèrent quatre de compagnie' (p.133), thereby effecting a link that is apparently oblique but which will soon furnish connexions. These on occasion enhance the facility with which clarity and complexity coexist, such as in I, viii when, after recalling the core troupe of *dramatis personae* assembled to date, the figures of Roquebrune and, vitally, Ragotin are added to the company. Furthermore, consistency is shown between the description of Le Destin's nocturnal ride through a village where the dogs are barking in II, i in pursuit of Angélique, and the account of her abduction in II, xi in which she recalls: 'ils se détournèrent autant qu'ils purent de tous les villages qu'ils trouvèrent, à la réserve d'un hameau dont je réveillai tous les habitants par mes cris' (p.260). Equally, certain comic or sentimental motifs subtend many of the episodes, in particular the unrequited love of Ragotin for L'Etoile, and the rivalry beween Roquebrune and La Rancune for the attentions of Inézille.

At the same time, Scarron is adept in the provision of potential. Thus, for example, after the members of the troupe and its extension have been established in the first book, the figures of the 'opérateur' and his wife arrive at the hostelry. Their first appearance is brief (although it features in the chapter heading of I, xv) and leads straight into a secondary narration, but they will play an increasingly important function, he as a comic trickster and she as the narrator of two of the Spanish stories. As characters are recalled, there may also be development of information about them, at the same time as a reminder that the implied reader should have been paying attention at their first appearance: '[le] mari d'Inézille, l'opérateur Ferdinando Ferdinandi, Normand se disant Vénitien (comme je vous ai déjà dit), médecin spagirique de profession et, pour dire franchement ce qu'il était, grand charlatan et encore plus grand fourbe' (p.317). Elsewhere we encounter prolepsis, such as when the Bouvillon episode of II, x is implicitly anticipated in the remark that 'Madame Bouvillon […] avait aussi son dessein' of II, viii (p.250).

A further intensificaton of the lack of forward dynamic, and a variant on the theme of retrospection, is afforded by the persistent use of the *in medias res* device (a characteristic *romanesque* and epic formula), whereby explanation follows rather than preceding incident, inviting Serroy's analogy with a detective novel (*32*, p.493). This way of introducing a story is already practised at the beginning of the work, and it is not until I, viii that the real background necessary for the understanding of the novel's opening is given, as the chapter title suggests: 'Dans lequel on verra plusieurs choses nécessaires à savoir pour l'intelligence du présent livre'. But the device is then carried on through the remainder of the text and, on several occasions when a new character is introduced, as we have seen, it will first be by his role, and only later by his name (true in particular for Roquebrune, for a long time simply referred to as 'le poète' and La Garouffière, equally introduced and developed as 'le jeune conseiller de Rennes'). The most extreme case of this is in the story of Le Destin and L'Etoile, at the end of which it is revealed that the character so far called Léonore is in fact L'Etoile (I, xviii). Elsewhere we are frequently faced with a sudden interruption, usually of a violent kind, as effect precedes cause, most surreally of all as Le Destin is telling the second part of his story: 'Le Destin continuait ainsi son histoire, quand on ouït tirer dans la rue un coup d'arquebuse et tout aussitôt jouer des orgues' (p.159). Eventually an explanation is given, although this may be some considerable time later. In this example, furthermore, the bewilderment is shared by the fictional participants: 'enfin tous les facétieux de l'hôtellerie se réjouirent sur la musique sans que pas un d'eux pût deviner celui qui la donnait et encore moins à qui ni pourquoi' (p.160). And, over an even longer time-scale, the words pronounced by Doguin at his (very early and sudden) death in I, vi (the event is noted in the chapter title), do not receive a satisfactory explanation until a remark made *en passant* in II, xv (p.302).

The same procedure is extended to the actors' narratives. Thus in I, xv, for example, the narrator (here Le Destin) seeks enlightenment, and then remarks: 'Ce que nous dit mademoiselle de Saldagne ne m'éclaircit pas entièrement, mais au moins aida-t-elle beaucoup à me faire deviner à peu près de quelle façon la chose était arrivée' (p.152). And again, later in the same chapter, he anticipates the reaction of his listeners: 'Vous êtes peut-être en peine de savoir comment mademoiselle de Léri se trouvait dans le jardin quand son frère nous y surprit, elle qui n'y était point venue comme avait fait sa sœur' (p.155). Later again, curiosity as to an unsolved mystery is expressed within the text by Le Destin: '"Il y a quelque mystère ici que je ne comprends point"' (p.268) in advance of L'Etoile's clarification. So this same mode of progression typifies the novel as a whole, and with a variety of players confused by the incidents. On occasion, the implied reader may simply be taunted by the narrator; at other points all the characters present at a given moment may be bewildered by an event which is occurring; and even, at the limits of the device, the narrator himself will claim that he too is awaiting enlightenment.

Returning to the structure of the primary narrative, we might attend first to the ways in which Scarron ends chapters. Certain examples end on a note of resolution, indicating the conclusion of an episode or a stage in the development: 'le charretier déchargea le bagage comique et s'en retourna à son village' (p.71); or with a hint of even greater domestic security: 'chacun regagna son lit et crut ce qu'il voulut de l'aventure, et la chèvre fut renfermée avec ses petits chiens' (p.74). A development of this effect is that of the coda, such as in I, xiii, after the long first part of the history of Le Destin, whose inception had been interrupted some twenty pages earlier by a fight emanating from Roquebrune's poetry, which closes the chapter thus: 'ce qui restait de la nuit se passa fort paisiblement dans l'hôtellerie, le poète par bonheur n'ayant point enfanté de nouvelles stances' (p.132); the end of II, ii, which closes parenthetically on Ragotin reciting poetry, believed by some peasants to be a vagrant preacher: 'Tandis qu'il récita, ils eurent toujours la tête nue et le respectèrent comme un prédicateur de grands chemins' (p.219); or finally, as the troupe is reassembling in Le Mans, the postscript at the end of II, xv, neatly signing off one of Scarron's great comic cameos: 'Pour la Bouvillon, elle fit la malade plus qu'elle ne l'était pour ne point recevoir l'adieu du comédien dont elle n'était pas satisfaite' (p.303). At certain points the chapter endings create an impression of only partial closure, offering the reader a sense of a succession of episodes, more or less mysterious in their interaction, until a late point in their evolution. This serves simply to reinforce the sense of finality at their dénouement, such as in the eventual ending of the stretcher-bearing episodes, tied in with the account of a hunt:

> Le curé s'en retourna à Domfront sans aucune mauvaise rencontre où, tant qu'il vivra, il contera son enlèvement. Le cheval mort fut mangé des loups ou des mâtins; le corps de celui qui avait été tué fut enterré je ne sais où; et La Rappinière, Le Destin, La Rancune et L'Olive, les archers et le prisonnier, s'en retournèrent au Mans. Et voilà le succès de la chasse de La Rappinière et des comédiens qui prirent un homme au lieu de prendre un lièvre. (pp.136-37)

Alternatively, a chapter may end on a downbeat, inviting a regain of impetus in the following opening. Thus I, xvii, devoted to a single comic mechanism, concludes in a sober way, preparing for the conclusion to the Le Destin story which opens the following one: 'L'heure du souper vint; on soupa dans l'hôtellerie. Chacun prit parti après le souper et Le Destin s'enferma avec les comédiennes pour continuer son histoire' (p.167); or concluding a similarly self-contained episode (II, vi) on a *sententia*: 'quand on attend quelqu'un avec impatience, les plus sages sont assez sots pour regarder souvent du côté qu'il doit venir' (p.239). Finally the narrator may tease the implied reader by an extension of the non-omniscience claim: 'Je ne dirai point si les comédiens plurent autant aux dames du Mans que les comédiennes avaient fait aux hommes' (p.165), to which implicit question an equally implicit answer is in fact afforded in II, x. Or, leading through non-omniscience to non-performance:

> Je n'ai pas su de quelle façon La Baguenodière fut
> accommodé avec les deux frères, tant il y a qu'il le fut;
> du moins n'ai-je ouï dire qu'ils se soient depuis rien fait
> les uns aux autres. Et voilà ce qui troubla en quelque
> façon la première représentation que firent nos
> comédiens devant l'illustre compagnie qui se trouvait
> lors dans la ville du Mans. (p.317)

Waugh brings these points together most succinctly (ironically
enough speaking explicitly of 'modern fiction') when she describes
two features: the tendency to 'begin by plunging in *in medias res*,
and end with the sense that nothing is finished, that life flows on'
(*33*, p.29).

Ingenious structural features are equally in evidence in the
links between chapters. The author persona frequently draws
attention to his activity, by a range of fairly standard but strongly
self-conscious formulae, concluding on occasion simply: 'je finirai
par là mon sixième chapitre' (p.239); using the variant of self-
restraint: 'Mais il n'y a que trop longtemps que je vous ennuie de la
débauche de Ragotin' (p.110); promising the continuation of a story
already begun: 'ils étaient dans un grand chemin aisé à suivre et qui
les conduisait en un village où nous les allons faire arriver dans le
suivant chapitre' (p.267); developing one: 'Là-dessus deux hommes
entrèrent dans le logis [...] desquels nous parlerons plus amplement
dans le suivant chapitre' (p.81); incorporating stasis in one narrative
strand with movement in another: 'Nous le laisserons reposer dans sa
chambre et nous verrons dans le suivant chapitre ce qui se passait en
celle des comédiens' (p.83); and with comic periphrasis (for
Ragotin's attempts to remove a chamber pot from his foot): 'Nous le
laisserons foulant l'étain d'un pied superbe pour aller recevoir un
train qui entra en même temps dans l'hôtellerie' (p.246). Finally, and
representing the cleanest break of all, is the introduction of the
interpolated story: 'Il [...] lut au Destin [...] une historiette qu'il avait
traduite de l'espagnol, que vous allez lire dans le suivant chapitre'
(p.271).

The same kinds of formula may begin chapters: 'Il vous
souviendra, s'il vous plaît, que dans le précédent chapitre, l'un de

ceux qui avaient enlevé le curé de Domfront avait quitté ses
compagnons et s'en était allé au galop je ne sais où' (p.137), skilfully
drawing out one strand of the narrative which has been left open for
development at the end of the previous chapter. Elsewhere a chapter
may begin with a fresh start, such as when the troupe returns to Le
Mans towards the end of the second volume: 'Le Destin et L'Etoile,
Léandre et Angélique, deux couples de beaux et parfaits amants,
arrivèrent dans la capitale du Maine sans faire de mauvaise
rencontre' (p.312). Continuity is thus created between chapters by a
self-conscious authorial presence rather than by narrative
sequentiality, both underscoring and resolving the complicated
structure of the work as a whole. Vitally too, certain such passages of
transition allow for the non-composition of a more conventional
novel to be sketched in alongside the novel that is being written. The
opening of I, xx in particular offers a glimpse of a conventional
digression on fortune, which the author persona then eschews in
order to get on with his story: 'il s'en faut prendre à la fortune sur les
caprices de laquelle j'aurais un beau champ pour m'étendre si je
n'étais obligé en conscience de le [Ragotin] tirer vitement du péril où
il se trouve' (p.182).

    In all these ways we see the process of our critical response
moving from an impression of chaos, to the discovery of a pattern or
balance that leads us to discern a certain degree of organization,
before this in turn reveals that, even here, there will be loose ends.
(These may of course have simply been awaiting resolution in the
third part.) It is almost as if the arbitrariness of the construction is
deliberately being emphasized by the apparently equally arbitrary
development or abandonment of particular episodes, so that we are
perpetually unsure as to whether we are dealing with a randomness
which seeks to bring us closer to a mimetic idea of realism or with a
stylized asymmetry. Perhaps in fact both are happening so that, in the
middle of the seventeenth century, the aims of the novelist Edouard
in Gide's *Les Faux-Monnayeurs* were already being realized:
'Présenter d'une part la réalité, présenter d'autre part l'effort pour la
styliser' (*10*, p.1081).

5. *Structure (ii): the* romanesque

Within the framework I have described, there exist two quite distinct strands of retrospective narrative. Most autonomously, and progressively more so, we have the interpolated Spanish stories (which may also contain, as does II, xiv, further internal narrative sub-divisions), increasingly encompassing the highest degree of narrative decorum, as well as the broadest time scale. These are also narrated, as the complexity of the novel increases, by characters who are the most independent, but who have 'un rapport [...] de "consanguinité"' (*32*, p.477). Giraud also notes, paradoxically, of these that 'le style écrit fleurit surtout dans les nouvelles espagnoles, pourtant placés dans la bouche d'un narrateur' (*4*, p.29) – although we note that they are predominantly read – just as the *récit cadre* seeks to convey orality, as a glimpse at the beginning of I, ii (p.67) and many other chapter openings will quickly show. Secondly we have the structurally more integrated narrations of the actors, lying thematically somewhere between the *récit cadre* and the Spanish stories, in which their past adventures are gradually revealed both to their fictional companions and to the empirical readers of the novel.

The Spanish stories

In order to assess their role in the work's evolution as fully as possible, I shall look at the Spanish stories in the order in which they occur in the text. The first, interestingly enough, is narrated by Ragotin, against the better judgement of his listeners, and includes the highest degree of consistency with the features of the primary narrative, together with the strong insistence by the narrator that he will not imitate the style of the newly-introduced 'petit fou': 'Vous allez voir cette histoire dans le suivant chapitre, non telle que la conta Ragotin, mais comme je la pourrai conter d'après un des auditeurs qui me l'a apprise. Ce n'est donc pas Ragotin qui parle, c'est moi' (p.86). Thus we find an early interruption by the primary narrator in the form of a disquisition on 'sottise' (p.87), together with various ironic asides, including an appearance of the claim of non-omniscience: 'Ils se dirent encore cent belles choses, que je ne vous dirai point, parce que je ne les sais pas' (p.88). However, the status of this must now be subtly more complex, since the story is an interpolated fiction. Is the primary narrator introducing a lacuna in his sources, or is he simply transferring a narrative habit from the primary text to the secondary? Or again, as would on occasions appear to be the case, is he narrating a claim of non-omniscience by the reported narrator? There is no need to answer these questions; just to be aware of the games of narration being played with the implied reader in and through the multiple layers of mediation. They add a freshness and spontaneity to the narration and, vitally, maintain the texture of the novel, whose complexity we are now able to grasp. The story is told immediately after the chapter in which the core group has been established; and it is as if the number of the novel's strands can be increased, with some conviction in the implied reader's commitment and attention now in place. The narration is in other respects well paced, clarifying the complexity without disguising it; and Ragotin's story is well received, even though it is not long after its conclusion (indeed just one sentence) before he is re-established as a figure of fun.

But what is the function of this story? In some ways, it is little more than a good yarn, but one in which certain conventions of the French *romanesque*, by being parodied, are immediately shown to be separate from the narrator's own concerns, either in his own right or as an introducer of other narratives. In a long caricature, taking the form of a single sentence paralipsis ('Je ne vous dirai point ...'), a parody of the *romanesque* is introduced within the story being narrated, and it is sufficiently striking as to be quoted *in extenso*:

> Je ne vous dirai point exactement s'il avait soupé et s'il
> se coucha sans manger, comme font quelques faiseurs de
> romans qui règlent toutes les heures du jour de leurs

héros, les font lever de bon matin, conter leur histoire
jusqu'à l'heure du dîner, dîner fort légèrement et après
dîner reprendre leur histoire ou s'enfoncer dans un bois
pour y parler tout seul, si ce n'est quand ils ont quelque
chose à dire aux arbres et aux rochers; à l'heure du
souper, se trouver à point nommé dans le lieu où l'on
mange, où ils soupirent et rêvent au lieu de manger, et
puis s'en vont faire des châteaux en Espagne sur quelque
terrasse qui regarde la mer, tandis qu'un écuyer révèle
que son maître est un tel, fils d'un roi tel et qu'il n'y a
pas de meilleur prince au monde et qu'encore qu'il soit
pour lors le plus beau des mortels, qu'il était encore tout
autre chose devant que l'amour l'eût défiguré. (p.90)

Parody, as Waugh suggests, 'fuses creation with critique' (*33*, p.68),
thus one novelistic tradition is being formed at the same time that
another is being rejected. Further, 'Scarron ne condamne pas en
principe le romanesque, et [...] même est très convaincu de
l'existence d'une bonne et d'une mauvaise façon d'écrire des romans
et des nouvelles' (*23*, p.172). The features enumerated will thus be
eschewed, and straight after the break the narrator continues his story
in a sharply contrasting style: 'Pour revenir à mon histoire, dom
Carlos se trouva le lendemain à son poste' (p.90). Bathetic asides
however continue to puncture the fiction: 'J'oubliais à vous dire que
je crois qu'il se lava la bouche, car j'ai su qu'il avait grand soin de
ses dents' (p.95), before the story is resolved by a kind of
'casuistique sentimentale', giving a peculiarly elegant twist to the
whole. But the strongest impression is still of an *exercice de style*,
rather than a moral enquiry; we are not being invited to meditate on
love and justice, as De Armas would claim (*36*, p.91), but on style
and play: self-consciousness and cleverness are primary, nowhere
more so than in this very first set piece.

   The first story of Inézille (I, xxii) finds a further company of
avid listeners, as well as occurring immediately after the powerful
advocacy of the genre by the 'jeune conseiller de Rennes', La
Garouffière (I, xxi); and again the primary narrator takes over the

narrative, now in order to compensate for the inadequate French of the secondary one. Consistency of register is thus (paradoxically) achieved, but with certain of the same ambiguities as in the story of Ragotin: some interventions seem to emanate from the primary narrator, in particular that which describes the function of 'duègnes', in terms characteristic of his idiom, as 'animaux rigides et fâcheux, aussi redoutés pour le moins que des belles-mères' (p.191); some from Inézille: 'Victoria [...] fit paraître ses cheveux, que l'on m'a assuré avoir été des plus beaux' (p.198); yet others could be attributed to either: 'Je ne m'amuserai point à vous dire les caresses que ces jeunes amants se firent' (p.202 – alongside a variety of more minor asides, comic euphemisms and *précieux* metonyms). Irrespective of the origins of such devices, their inclusion again allows the texture of the tale to remain broadly similar to the primary narrative as to Ragotin's story, if different in its emphases, and, once again, to retain its lightness of touch. As Hainsworth comments:

> Aucune de ces interpolations n'étant autorisée, bien entendu, par les textes originaux, il ressort donc que Scarron, tout en réformant, d'une part, suivant les tendances mêmes du genre, la nouvelle espagnole, l'affuble d'autre part de toutes les grâces du style burlesque, et lui donne un air comique dont il n'y a pas la moindre trace chez Castillo Solórzano ou María de Zayas [his Spanish originals]. (*23*, p.183)

Characteristic of its genre and country of origin, it deals with questions of honour, with disguise, betrayal and intrigue, and leads to a happy outcome, with a tone of optimism prevalent: 'plus que toute autre chose, un reste de générosité [...] s'était conservé dans l'âme de dom Fernand' (p.204), again affording a parallel with the spirit of the primary narrative. *Points de repère* are also provided to guide the listener (and thus implied reader) through the complexities of the plot, alongside certain minor thematic features which also reflect the primary text: the occurrence of 'brancards'; and an important episode which takes place before a theatrical performance. These again may be no more than coincidences; and yet their motivic status in the primary text marks them out. As so often with Scarron, we simply cannot be sure; yet such parallels do lend support to De Armas's view that the stylistic changes effected by Scarron to his Spanish intertexts 'bring the *nouvelles* interpolated in the *Roman comique* to resemble the rest of the text, so that the reader finds no abrupt transition between the adventures of Ragotin and those of Dom Carlos' (*36*, p.80). Most importantly, however, and in parallel with Ragotin's story, what is discussed at the opening of the following chapter is not the moral of the story, but its mode of narration. It is thus enclosed in an aesthetic debate and therefore, once again, claims our attention as a narrative entity rather than as a specifically cautionary tale.

The third Spanish story occurs in the second part, and is narrated to Le Destin by La Garouffière, 'qui prétendait fort au bel esprit' (p.271). The setting is divided between Africa and Spain (with the intervention of a 'comte napolitain'); the element of *pittoresque* is high, with emphasis on the barbarity of Moorish customs; and, importantly, it contains subsidiary narratives, so that the interpolated story here reflects by its own interpolations the structure of the overall text in a kind of chiasmus (ABCBA), leading through a double retrospection to the present moment of narration. Furthermore the narratives within the secondary narration contain a higher proportion of direct speech; and although asides, commentaries and *sententiae* are still present, they are now more or less unambiguously attributed to the secondary narrator (pp.272-73). Despite the tale's multilayered nature, therefore, it presents a high degree of fluency, and its narration by La Garouffière (it is again read out, in conformity with its complexity) confirms this impression.

The violence of the primary narrative is also as, if not more, present in the interpolated stories, not just in individual episodes, but, as is appropriate to the Spanish context, in a code of honour and its defence and in the frequent departures on to the battlefield or to sea, for a multiplicity of motives (disappointment in love, disgrace, concealment and so on). Thematically the motifs of amorous intrigue, jealousies, wicked parents, abduction and escape, elopement and trickery, secret rendez-vous, mistaken identity, honour codes, fights, battles, storms and swordsmanship all recur, to which is crucially added in the third tale the yet more exaggeratedly *romanesque* device of a transvestite disguise. Even (or especially) in this respect however a note of irony cuts on occasion through the adventures, as the narrator corrects himself: 'ce cavalier [...] [prit] parti avec lui, je veux dire avec elle' (p.294), taking a more developed form as the disguise is dropped. This cliff-hanger, at the limits of *vraisemblance*, reaches a highly complex dénouement in which the loose ends are meticulously tied up, and establishes itself therefore as the most autonomous, the most internally consistent and arguably the most independently exciting of the interpolated narratives, an impression reinforced retrospectively by the highly fragmented nature of the chapter immediately following (II, xv). We find therefore an authentic and convincing *romanesque* finally emerging as an option within the text, and indeed, the balance and coherence of La Garouffière's story contrast saliently with the superficial randomness of the primary narrative (a remark which would not however lead me to agree with Muratore's assertion that 'the embedded fictions appear to the reader as intrusive supplements inserted to frustrate the reader's progress and break his concentration', *28*, p.105)[5]. On the contrary, 'en résistant aux abondantes invraisemblances et complications que lui proposent ses modèles, Scarron a su manifester son originalité et s'orienter, à sa manière, non pas vers la démesure baroque, mais vers la raison classique' (*35*, p.252).

Finally we have the second story of Inézille in the penultimate chapter (II, xix), read before the whole company after a dinner given by Ragotin. The setting is now Seville, although here again there is a geographical extension to the Spanish territories of Flanders, Naples

---

[5] Muratore indeed seems to represent a particular view of the novel, whereby readers 'labor in vain to uncover a connecting thread that might fuse inner and outer fictions' (*28*, p.108), in opposition to the more integrational readings, especially of De Armas, for whom the novel 'blends [...] the different aspects of life into a cohesive whole' (*37*, p.92). The term I have introduced to escape from such a critical impasse is 'texture', a metaphor which will perhaps allow for a multiplicity of threads (Muratore's metonym) to be woven into a complex pattern.

and Sicily. The *entrée en matière* is extended and convoluted, and incorporates substantial passages of dialogue; it leads in turn to a long intervention by the narrator, Inézille (herself now an established figure in the primary narrative), which incorporates the reflexion on the comic *topos* of 'vieilles prudes' (p.323) and a comparison between French and Spanish manners; and this is itself followed by a discussion by the two sisters of the story on the rights and wrongs of marriage. In addition to the sententious and explanatory facets of the story, it is again notable for its deployment of many of the same themes as the other Spanish and retrospective narratives; even names (Dorothée, Dom Carlos) and places (Naples) recur; and the plot again ends on a double (indeed triple) marriage. It is also remarkable for its stylistic variety, incorporating as it does dialogue, poetry and letters; and the tone is at times lightened here as elsewhere by moments of comic irony, thus in the unmasking of amorous self-delusion:

> Il m'est plus indifférent que haïssable, lui dit Féliciane
> et, si je vous ai dit qu'il me déplaisait, ç'a été plutôt par
> quelque complaisance que j'ai voulu avoir pour vous que
> par une véritable aversion que j'eusse pour lui. – Avouez
> plutôt, ma chère sœur, lui répondit Dorothée, que vous
> ne me parlez pas ingénument. (p.334)

Alongside these features, it again takes up certain devices characteristic of the narrator of the primary level. Stylistically we find comic euphemism (p.326), and portraiture (p.327); and at the metafictional level (albeit now unambiguously attributed to the secondary narrator), non-omniscience: 'Je ne vous ferai point voir ici de leurs billets amoureux, car il n'en est point tombé entre mes mains' (p.326); sententiousness, based appropriately enough on a Spanish proverb: 'On dit que l'amour, le feu et l'argent ne se peuvent longtemps cacher' (p.326); spontaneity: 'Ce cavalier (je me viens de souvenir qu'il s'appelait dom Diègue)' (p.327); explanations: 'la plupart des romances de Séville, ce qui est à Paris des chansons de Pont-Neuf' (p.327); asides: '(si je l'ose ainsi dire)' (p.327); ambiguity of motivation: 'remarquant sa sœur si changée, ou qui feignait de l'être' (p.333); and most strikingly of all a contemporary theatrical simile: 'sans répandre leur sang comme Pyrame et Thisbé' (p.326), effecting thereby the clearest link between Spanish past and theatrical present, and so anchoring once and for all the secondary narrative in the primary. The Spanish stories in this way chart a progression towards an authentic *romanesque* while at the same time assimilating certain features of the primary narrative. The reader is not, *pace* Muratore, 'laboring' to identify common features; on the contrary, as I hope I have shown, '[Scarron] était, on le sait, un hispaniste des plus convaincus [...]. Il ne faut pas oublier cependant que tous ses ouvrages, et quelle que soit leur source, portent la marque d'un génie qui lui est très personnelle' (*23*, p.171).

The actors' narratives

The second category of interpolated narration is afforded by the retrospective narratives of the actors: Le Destin and L'Etoile in Book I (xiii, xv, xviii); La Caverne (II, iii); and Léandre and Angélique (II, v), constantly expanding our view of pre-narrative time, and introducing their adventurous pasts into the more down-to-earth presents of their lives. These form the second obviously *romanesque* elements of the *Roman comique*, although Lever points rightly in this context to 'le décalage entre une conception romanesque de l'existence et les contingences matérielles qui la contrarient' (*26*, p.157). As Bénac remarks, 'les trois récits reposent sur la même technique imitée de la nouvelle espagnole: le mélange habile de réalité et de fiction' (*2*, p.47); and for Serroy: 'les récits sont [...] au point de jonction de la réalité et du romanesque' (*32*, p.475). It is symptomatic therefore that they are predominantly retrospective, implying that the present is by definition more mundane than the past, since the most vivid of the dramatic and amorous episodes have affected those involved in them before the chronological period of the primary narrative, as is exemplified in the revelation of the identity of L'Etoile: 'Mademoiselle de L'Etoile prit la parole et dit que sa compagne avait raison de douter qu'elle fût cette Léonore dont Le Destin avait fait une beauté de roman' (pp.171-72). The

break with the past is clear, and the *romanesque*, we are thereby led
to understand, is no longer 'actuel'. It does however exist as part of a
continuum, and figures from it (typically villainous ones) continue to
lurk in the background of the primary narrative. As De Armas
accurately notes, 'even in the present action, there are the usual
kidnappings and recognitions of the heroic romances' (*36*, p.66); or
for Muratore, 'Destin's account represents [...] a kind of narrative
compromise, an ideal hybridization of the real author's [?] narrative
manner and the fictional maker of the embedded tales' (*28*, p.114).
Soon after the novel's opening, a mysterious past is evoked (indeed
the bizarre physical appearance of Le Destin at the very outset leads
to some questions being asked), and the implied reader's curiosity is
mediated in turn through that of La Rancune: '"il ne découvre point
qui il est, ni d'où il est, non plus qu'une belle Cloris qui
l'accompagne [L'Etoile], qu'il appelle sa sœur"' (p.75). Further dark
hints then come from the narrator (e.g. p.81), and, as mysterious
coincidences succeed one another, so the sense of a plot (in both
meanings of the term) evolves, to be resolved more often than not
only to leave further questions unanswered. At other points, such as
in II, iv ('Le Destin trouve Léandre'), various loose ends are
gradually tied up, while the absence of Angélique remains
mysterious. In these ways, certain strands are left in abeyance, while
others find resolution, and yet more are introduced with a potential
for future development.

  The story of Le Destin and L'Etoile is arranged in a disparate
tripartite structure in the first book, whereby the first and third parts
(chapters xiii and xviii) embrace the second (xv). The first part is
amply prepared for in the chapter which leads into it (I, xii), with the
reader appetized by passing hints: 'La Caverne [...] reprocha à Destin
et à L'Etoile que, depuis le temps qu'ils étaient ensemble [...] ils
avaient eu si peu de confiance en elle et en sa fille qu'elles ignoraient
encore leur véritable condition' (p.113). The implied reader, thus
represented by La Caverne and Angélique, awaits with impatience
the clarification of their origins, even though a violent interruption
and its subsidence further delay, as so often, the narration. After so
much turmoil, he then joins the fictive listeners (whose presence is

periodically acknowledged in the course of the narration, and whose identity is significantly stable throughout the three parts of the story) in a desire for calm and for enlightenment.

Le Destin's narration succeeds particularly well, in common with the Spanish stories, in maintaining a lightness of touch, especially in the context of his loveless childhood, a fact helped by the rapid inclusion of two comic anecdotes about the meanness of his father (creating thereby a degree of formal diversity within the digression), and a self-mocking depiction of a tongue-tied performance by himself at a dinner in the company of Léonore: 'Si la mère n'eût toujours parlé, le dîner se fût passé à la chartreuse' (p.126). Furthermore the inept letter written to Léonore by the lovelorn narrator is laughable in its clichéd passion (pp.128-29). In the 'Suite de l'histoire' a similar element of the comic potential of the sentimental is afforded in the laborious dialogue between Le Destin and Léonore, litotically described after a sequence of sterile exchanges as 'une conversation qui ne me conduisait pas assez vite où je voulais aller' (p.141); and the mawkish death-wish of the narrating hero, 'je fis tout ce que je pus pour me faire tuer' (p.142), points as well to an awareness within the older narrator of the absurdity of the excesses of adolescent passion. This potential is then taken into the Verville episodes, with Le Destin's comic anticipation of a conversation with (as he believes) a servant girl, 'qui m'allait demander sans doute combien je gagnais de gages, quelles servantes je connaissais dans le quartier, si je savais des chansons nouvelles et si j'avais bien des profits avec mon maître' (p.144), leading in turn into a parody of a lovers' quarrel: '"Tu veux dire, reprit-elle, que je suis peut-être laide. Hé, monsieur le difficile, ne sais-tu pas bien que la nuit tous les chats sont gris?"' (p.145) and so on. Verville's own account of his *amours* becomes tedious: 'il me tint toute la nuit à redire cent fois les mêmes choses' (p.146); and the strategies for meetings end up with a valet 'dans une garde-robe' and the heroine 'dans un petit cabinet' (pp.146-47) leading to a no less farcical escape (p.148). Le Destin also shares with the primary narrator an occasional barbed aside, most memorably when they are travelling from Orléans to Paris, of how Mademoiselle de La Boissière, 'que la joie de n'être plus sans argent avait guérie plutôt qu'autre chose, se trouva assez forte pour aller en carrosse' (p.173). Overall, just as with the primary narrative, grave episodes are handled with a disarming levity, and in this way again, the texture of the work remains constant across the range of narrative levels.

Irony is present too in the *larmoyant* introduction to the (briefer) first part of the 'Histoire de La Caverne' (which is incidentally never finished) of whom we read that 'La Caverne ne pouvait souffrir alors que quelqu'un se dît plus malheureux qu'elle' (p.219); and, despite her misfortunes, she too acknowledges as she relates the story of the page who forgets his couplet: 'Quelque grand sujet que j'aie d'être fort triste, je ne puis songer à ce jour-là que je ne rie de la plaisante façon dont le grand page s'acquitta de son rôle' (p.223), even if the same man then goes on to kill her father (an event reported however without any emotion on p.225). And the touching dénouement of Léandre's story and the ensuing vows of fidelity by Le Destin are soon broken off by the sound of 'une grande rumeur' and by its sequel (p.235). Yet whilst these more abrupt tonal changes intensify the texture, they do not destroy it. To use another metaphor, the colours of the whole picture sharpen at such moments, but do not threaten its unity.

Clarity of writing within apparent confusion is also carried over from the primary narrative, and we notice how the 'hideux chaos' which can occur in it is reflected in the 'grande confusion' (p.153) of the interpolated story. Furthermore the nature of the revelations about Le Destin's father which are to ensue clearly requires some defence of their veracity, and they are thus preluded by the epithets: 'très difficiles à croire, et néanmoins très véritables' (p.117). The geographical *cadre* is here, as with the Spanish stories, extended (initially to Scotland, then to Rome); and an element of the more overtly *pittoresque* in precision of locality (churches, gardens, districts) is now closer to the surface. Coincidences, here as in the Spanish stories, are rife, although in both cases within the realms of the (tenuously) credible; and characters, typically good or bad, remain within a quickly established moral status. Several further thematic features then unite the two strands of interpolated narrative, and specific parallels are easy to enumerate: mother / daughter relationships, woundings, bravery on the battlefield, disguises, mistaken identities, recognitions, obstacles and ruses for their removal, swordsmanship, thefts and clandestine meetings.

What thematically characterizes the actors' narrations in particular is the omnipresence of a certain elevation of feelings. This may occur between lovers within a social class, such as in the courtship of Léandre and Angélique: 'à force de l'aimer, je l'engageai à m'aimer autant que je l'aimais' (p.233), or in the discovery by Verville and Mlle de Saldagne that they are both members of a higher rank, thereby demonstrating that true affective and social compatibility will prevail despite disguises and obstacles. Alternatively the capacity for true feelings may transcend class barriers: thus although Le Destin benefits both from a noble 'parrain' and protector, his own origins are in fact lowly (as are those of Léonore), yet his demeanour belies his status. Finally, it may unite people of the same sex, so that, as Léandre finishes his story, Le Destin speaks with feeling: '"Faites la comédie avec nous; vous n'êtes pas seul qui la ferez et qui pourrriez faire quelque chose de meilleur [...]. Cependant je vivrai avec vous comme un frère"' (pp.234-35); and, in turn, '[Léandre] le remercia [...] et lui fit des protestations d'amitié si tendres qu'il en fut aimé dès ce temps-là autant qu'un honnête homme le peut être d'un autre' (p.235). As Bénac comments, 'même dans un humble décor, [peuvent] fleurir les sentiments les plus délicats' (*2*, p.148) (and equally, if more rarely, the sentimental is present in the primary narrative, such as in the conclusion of II, xv); and Coulet notes that 'même le roman comique, qui s'oppose au roman idéaliste et le ridiculise, ne peut se passer du romanesque noble dans ses épisodes sérieux' (*20*, p.139).

The greatest textu(r)al integration comes on the other hand in the second part of the 'Histoire de Destin et de L'Etoile', couched as it is itself within a tripartite chapter: 'Arrivée d'un opérateur dans l'hôtellerie. Suite de l'histoire de Destin et de L'Etoile. Sérénade'. This embedding of what is in fact a tenuously connected sub-plot of the Le Destin story (the Verville episode), within a chapter of primary narrative brings the disparate levels as close to each other as they will ever come in the work, and thus blurs to the maximum the distinction between the *romanesque* and the real (and thus tacitly accords veracity to the fictions). Furthermore, despite the tenuous links, symmetries emerge between the two stories (Le Destin's and Verville's), which then conclude in a double marriage, with both the good and the wicked brother satisfied. The Verville / Saldagne axis is thereafter revived by La Garouffière in the chapter following (and indeed explaining) the abductions of Angélique (II, xi) and L'Etoile (II, xii and xiii); and the figure of Saldagne remains, too, as an ominous link with the actors' pasts, as Le Destin's story is brought to its conclusion in the narrative present moment: '"Si je ne me trompe, je ne serai pas longtemps en ce pays sans le trouver, ce que je crains moins pour moi que pour Léonore qui serait abandonnée d'un serviteur fidèle si elle me perdait ou si quelque malheur me séparait d'avec elle". Le Destin finit ainsi son histoire [...]' (p.177).

In addition to these stories we have two briefer and more recent retrospections, the stories of the abductions of Angélique (pp.260-62) and of L'Etoile (pp.268-69), in both cases now situated within a past contained within the time-scale of the primary fiction. Yet other stories are either promised but delayed (for ever, as it so transpires) – thus La Rancune's story of the poet is interrupted by its subject, and results in an aborted narrative after a promising *entrée en matière*: 'il s'en excusa, promettant de leur conter une autre fois la vie du poète tout entière et que celle de sa femme y serait comprise' (p.164); or implicitly contained within an encounter from which the reader is tantalizingly excluded, as the narrator prefers to pursue another strand: 'Je crois qu'il y eût eu bien du plaisir à les entendre [Léandre and Angélique], mais il vaut mieux pour eux que leur entrevue ait été secrète' (p.262). The fertility of the text is thus demonstrated and the potential for further digressions intimated, hypothetically at least, until the whole troupe has revealed its origins and those of its associates: the account of La Rancune's own incorporation into the troupe occurs late in the story of Le Destin (p.173); and perhaps even the shadowy figure of L'Olive would have been accorded a fuller profile, beyond his drinking and sleeping habits (e.g. p.218) and his periodic function as a straight man to a comic partner (e.g. p.216). In particular the figures of Inézille and the 'opérateur' seem to take on a high profile late in the second volume, in such a way as to suggest their potential for chapters to come, a potential that was indeed exploited in the *Suite de Préchac* (see Appendix I).

On the other hand, the business of *rattrapage*, when it is independent of the retrospective narratives of the actors, is accorded little (apparent) prestige by the author persona, giving as he does such titles to the chapters in question as 'Des moins divertissants du présent volume' (II, xi) and then straightaway 'Qui divertira peut-être aussi peu que le précédent' (II, xii) in the two chapters where the (not undramatic) 'enlèvement d'Angélique' is retrospectively narrated. It would seem fair to conclude from this that the business of plot invention is accorded a higher priority than that of plot resolution in the author persona's hierarchy, and to draw further evidence from it for the unimportance of the 'completed' novel. How the increasingly complex web of narratives and events is eventually resolved, we are led to understand, is of little intrinsic interest, and will indeed be of only provisional completeness.

In conclusion we might stress that the role of the listener in general fulfils a sympathetic function in the work, as well as facilitating the transition from one narrative level to the next. As even Muratore concedes (in her oddly ungenerous reading of the novel), 'the author [...] consistently records the overwhelming approval of the listeners at the conclusion of each tale' (*28*, p.107). After the initial scepticism confronting Ragotin, the fictional listeners become explicitly attentive, for example when we learn that 'La Caverne contait ainsi son histoire et L'Etoile l'écoutait attentivement' (p.228), or that 'Le Destin s'assit sur le pied du lit et Léandre lui dit ce que vous allez lire' (p.231). And among the company assembled to hear Angélique, even 'les moins curieux [...] eurent grande impatience d'apprendre de mademoiselle Angélique une aventure qui leur semblait si étrange' (p.259 – now in direct distinction to the implied reader who, it is predicted, will find the chapter 'Des moins divertissants du présent volume'). In the second part of Le Destin's story (I, xv), it is clearer that the relationship between Le Destin and his listeners on occasions reflects that of the primary narrator and the implied reader, in the use of reflecting devices, notably asides (e.g. p.148), choices of motivation (e.g. p.148) and hypothetical reactions: 'Vous êtes peut-être en peine de savoir [...]' (p.155). And the sympathetic role of the listeners is again stressed as they interrupt Le Destin as he moves towards the revelation of Léonore's identity as L'Etoile, and confirm that the dénouement was in accordance with their hopes, '"à cause que l'on a toujours de la peine à croire une chose que l'on a beaucoup désirée"' (p.172). A minor narration in reported speech by the local curé in II, vi is on the other hand more reluctantly received by his preoccupied listeners, but here the overall context of the narration lends itself best to this kind of scepticism (despite the objectively well-turned quality of the anecdote): 'Le Destin et Léandre ne s'émurent pas beaucoup du conte que le curé leur donnait pour bon, soit qu'ils ne le trouvassent pas si plaisant qu'il leur avait dit, ou qu'ils ne fussent pas alors en humeur de rire' (p.238 – and again note the option afforded in the motivation). What is rescued from the story as a result is the comic status of the curé as an inveterate and insensitive talker, since the narrative continues: 'Le curé, qui était grand parleur, n'en voulut pas demeurer là [...]' (ibid.).

It is by thus dealing with the structures of the text as a whole, their interplay and their variety, that we become increasingly aware of the complex aesthetic criteria which govern the project in its entirety. Adam makes the important point that the actors' narratives are in fact also imitations of the Spanish style of *romanesque*, of which purer examples abound elsewhere in the novel. Scarron has thus largely discarded the old-style French *romanesque*, concerned with distant times, with 'ces héros languissants, qui rêvent sur quelque terrasse au bord de la mer et qui soupirent vers quelque belle inaccessible' (*1*, p.38); and its exclusion is endorsed by the ironic references to it scattered throughout the text. The *romanesque* which replaces it is inspired by Spanish writing, in particular the *novelas cortas* [*nouvelles*], and is characterized by being situated within the feasible, and by its relative temporal proximity, even though it still involves 'des histoires ingénieuses et compliquées' (*1*, p.38). As

Coulet notes, 'par rapport [...] aux grands romans chevaleresques ou sentimentaux, la nouvelle espagnole représente un grand pas vers le réalisme' (*20*, p.206). The actors' narratives thus fulfil a function somewhere between 'l'actualité française' and 'le romanesque espagnol', and so once again point to the necessity of a multiple structure. It is as if the *romanesque*, by its contamination with the ordinariness of the actors' daily lives, has become a writable possibility.

Simon, in a fascinating article, sees the three narrative levels as corresponding to different conceptions of love: 'The treatment of love in the actors' world partakes of both the literary romanticism of the Spanish stories and of the crass realism of Ragotin's world; but it cannot be identified with either of these extremes. [...] Scarron thus makes his realistic portrayal of love depend on a subtly orchestrated interplay between three different levels of existence and narration' (*45*, pp.135-36). At the same time, as I have tried to suggest, there is an overall unity of texture, and any view of generic plurality in the *Roman comique* has to be held within this textu(r)al consistency. In order to reconcile these two positions, we may usefully turn in conclusion to Bénac, who proposes the most unified reading of the work: '[Scarron] a emprunté à la *novela corta* une théorie du romanesque qui s'étend à toute l'invention du *Roman comique*: un romanesque qui garde le mystère de l'intrigue et le charme des héros parfaits du roman précieux, mais sans trop s'écarter de la réalité à laquelle il demeure lié et d'où il tire toute sa vraisemblance et sa puissance d'émotion' (*2*, p.36).

6. The Author / Author Persona / Narrator

Such considerations must, inevitably, lead us into the metafictional domain, and to the account by the author / author persona / narrator of his activities, which allows for a parody of novelistic convention to be incorporated alongside the novel that is in the process of composition. Booth records (in fact of *Don Quijote*) the existence of 'a fully self-conscious narrator whose qualities determine the quality of his book in spite of his playfully professed desires' (*18*, p.166); and Rousset develops the point:

> L'interventionnisme impénitent de Scarron est à double entente: il nie d'un côté ce qu'il affirme de l'autre, il compromet la crédibilité d'une fiction dont il prétend garantir la réalité, il étale l'activité de l'auteur quand celui-ci déclare son désir de disparaître. Ce faisant, il reflète les difficultés et les tensions d'une esthétique romanesque qui se cherche entre l'imaginaire et le réel. (*44*, p.153)

As is true of so many of its features, the narrative mode of the *Roman comique* disconcerts the reader, and uncertainty prevails at several points both as to the status of the events narrated (as between those invented and those recorded) and thus as to their relationship to the author persona / narrator.

The author: Paul Scarron

If we begin by looking briefly at the historical figure of the author himself, we find in real life a colourful character, as we may infer from the self-portrait (pp.49-50). Paul Scarron was born in Paris in 1610. After taking minor religious orders, he joined the household of

the Bishop of Le Mans in 1633. In 1635 he accompanied his
employer to Rome and, on his return later the same year, became a
member of the cathedral chapter. In 1638, according to an anecdote,
he adopted a carnival disguise by covering his naked body in honey
and down; when exposed, he took refuge in the river, and stayed in
the freezing waters until he was able to return to the safety of his
house under cover of darkness. Whatever the truth of the story, the
rheumatic condition that ensued is historically attested, and Scarron
spent the remainder of his life in progressive stages of disability. As
he wrote of himself in 1648:

> Mes jambes et mes cuisses ont fait premièrement un
> angle obtus, et puis un angle égal, et enfin un aigu. Mes
> cuisses et mon corps en font un autre et, ma tête se
> penchant sur mon estomac, je ne représente pas mal un
> Z. J'ai les bras raccourcis aussi bien que les jambes, et
> les doigts aussi bien que les bras. Enfin, je suis un
> raccourci de la misère humaine. (p.50)

In 1640, he returned to Paris, to the Marais, and in 1643 there
appeared the *Recueil de quelques vers burlesques*. Further works in
the same vein preceded his first stage comedy, *Jodelet ou le Maître
valet* (1645), followed by *Les Trois Dorothées ou le Jodelet souffleté*,
also known as *Jodelet duelliste,* in 1647. The six books of the *Virgile
travesti en vers burlesques* appeared between 1648 and 1651, in
which year the first part of the *Roman comique* was printed. In 1652
he married Françoise d'Aubigné, eventually to become the Marquise
de Maintenon, and then Louis XIV's morganatic wife. (In her later
life, reminders of her humbler origins were often couched in the form
of references to her as 'la veuve Scarron'.) In 1647 a further play,
Dom Japhet d'Arménie was successfully premièred at the Hôtel de
Bourgogne, and published in 1653. In the following year, Scarron
and his wife took up residence in the rue Neuve-Saint-Louis, now rue
de Turenne, which became a meeting place for Parisian literary
society. Thereafter several more minor works accompanied the
Nouvelles tragi-comiques, adapted from Spanish sources, in 1655-

56, before the second part of the *Roman comique* was published in 1657. Scarron died in 1660. The historical Scarron intrudes explicitly into the novel at only one point, when his play *Dom Japhet* is performed in the *fêtes* at Le Mans in II, xvii, and the contrast between play and playwright is briefly resumed in the appositional phrase: '*Dom Japhet*, ouvrage de théâtre aussi enjoué que celui qui l'a fait a sujet de l'être peu' (p.314). To this we might add the two dedications (pp.57 and 211-12), which the historical Scarron addressed to his patrons.

The author persona

Turning to fictionally internal concerns, I should begin by noting that the presence of a first person fulfilling a dual persona as author and narrator has led me to use whichever term seemed the more appropriate in the context. I have therefore preferred 'author persona' at those (relatively rare) points where the 'je' adopts the tone and function of a creative inventor, or where the business of novelistic composition is dealt with; and used 'narrator' for the more frequent interventions of the teller of the story, including those moments at which claims of veracity and non-omniscience are deployed, and at which digressions and commentaries on the substance are included. Put another way, the author persona deals with how the story is told, the narrator with what is told. Reflecting this, I have used the term 'fictive reader' to designate the specified addressee of the author persona, and 'implied reader' when such a status is given to be understood by the narrator. However, such distinctions cannot be absolute, since the various functions, far from being totally separate, are differentiable largely by virtue of context and perspective (with shifts on occasion between the two within a single intervention); and since the ambiguous status of the 'je' between creator and recorder constitutes a fundamental element of the work's playfulness. The author persona who appears initially in the *Au lecteur* retires thereafter for a good deal of the time from the foreground, to be replaced by the narratorial and commentating one. And yet in the course of these functions, a periodically more authorial intrusion will recur.

In common with the opening dedication (p.57), the *Au lecteur scandalisé des fautes d'impression qui sont dans mon livre* (p.61 – a pretext previously used by Sorel) projects a strong impression of unworthiness of character, together with carelessness and haste of composition, and the same tone of hyperbolic modesty is taken up again in the dedication of the second part (pp.211-12). The fact that the author persona is ready to depict himself in these terms ties in well both with the historical Scarron and with certain other characteristics of the text: it makes him an appropriately sympathetic observer of and commentator on his equally (socially) modest creations; and it prepares us for the reiterated claims of informality and negligence which punctuate the narrative, even if the care with which carelessness is apparently achieved must point to these as being as much of a convention as the true description of a work method. The fictive reader is in turn treated, appropriately enough, with the same sort of familiarity reserved for Rabelais's 'beuveurs [et] verolez'. He is initially addressed as 'tu' (in distinction to the dedicatees, the Cardinal de Retz* and Mme Foucquet*, who are 'vouvoyés') and accorded a teasing disrespect, establishing thereby a kind of informal pact which will be recalled in subsequent narrations; and, more importantly, is subdivided according to temperament: 'Voilà, Lecteur Bénévole, ou Malévole, tout ce que j'ai à te dire' (p.61). The author persona thus involves himself in a game with his reader, who shares his initial discovery of the actors as 'nos inconnus' (p.66), and will write soon after of 'notre roman' (p.74).

The playfulness introduced in this pact and the presentation of the novel as nothing more than a set of *Errata* are then confirmed in the interruption of the first interpolated story, where it is again disparagingly described as 'un ramas de sottises' (p.87); and the same concerns are brought into the body of the text at the opening of I, xii. This important *entrée en matière* repeats the claims of carelessness in the light of the pact with the 'lecteur bénévole': 's'il est scandalisé de toutes les badineries qu'il a vues jusques ici dans le présent livre, il fera fort bien de n'en lire pas davantage' (p.111). It then goes on, via a brief jibe at a contemporary novel (*Cyrus*), to claim spontaneity through a well-tried simile (which was also to be used by Sévigné): 'je fais dans mon livre comme ceux qui mettent la bride sur le col de leurs chevaux', before concluding with a light-hearted (and quickly subverted) deliberation on whether or not the writer has a corrective purpose.

The same tone of *désinvolture* recurs in certain of the chapter headings, where the author persona, marked by 'un léger accent de scepticisme' (*20*, p.203), again points to the game being played with the fictive reader. This is especially true when they are misleading: I, v, entitled 'Qui ne contient pas grand-chose' is in fact packed with incident, whereas the following, purporting to contain many 'choses mémorables' in fact has very few. In addition he draws the reader's attention to the apparently frivolous nature of the whole enterprise by including the chapters entitled 'Des moins divertissants du présent volume' and 'Qui divertira peut-être aussi peu que le précédent' (II, xi and xii), both indeed chapters of *rattrapage*, but whose titles will of course paradoxically guarantee that the empirical reader is teased into reading them. In the links effected between chapters too, as we have seen, the emphasis is placed on spontaneity of composition, most explicitly at the beginning of the last part of the 'Histoire de Destin et de L'Etoile' (I, xviii): 'J'ai fait le précédent chapitre un peu court, peut-être que celui-ci sera plus long; je n'en suis pourtant pas bien assuré, nous allons voir' (p.167). As an extension of this feature, we find the problems of writing on occasion revealed on the surface of the text. In a particularly chaotic episode (II, vii), the author persona interrupts paraliptically: 'Il faudrait une meilleure plume que la mienne pour bien représenter les beaux coups de poing qui s'y donnèrent' (p.244). Elsewhere he tells of his efforts in composing a difficult, because particularly vigorous chapter (I, xix):

> Le méchant écuyer resserra les jambes et le cheval releva
> le cul encore plus fort, et alors le malheureux se trouva le
> pommeau entre les fesses, où nous le laisserons comme
> sur un pivot pour nous reposer un peu; car, sur mon

> honneur, cette description m'a plus coûté que tout le·
> reste du livre et encore n'en suis-je pas trop bien
> satisfait. (p.182)

Self-mocking sententiousness occurs at times, notably at the beginning of the chapter which follows the conclusion of Le Destin's story, as if to afford a more acerbic perspective on the sentimental emphasis established: 'L'amour, qui fait tout entreprendre aux jeunes et tout oublier aux vieux, qui a été cause de la guerre de Troie et de tant d'autres dont je ne veux pas prendre la peine de me ressouvenir [...]' (p.177); and, above all, in the intervention in II, x, which proceeds through a *sententia* on talkative people to some advice on how to deal with them ('c'est de parler autant et plus qu'eux'), to an ironic coda: 'J'appuie cette réflexion-là sur plusieurs expériences et même je ne sais si je ne suis point de ceux que je blâme' (p.256). At such points the consistently self-deflating authorial presence in the text, highly self-conscious and explicitly interventionist, is clearly distinct from a simpler narrative function.

At the same time, we would be misguided if we saw no degree of self-confidence, even arrogance in this presentation, since the character and opinions of the fictive reader are in fact indifferent to the author persona. Any ambivalence on the part of this reader towards the *vraisemblance* of episodes is of no concern to him, because the events recorded are claimed to be true. They are, after all, 'ces très véritables et très peu héroïques aventures' (p.111), with the implied denial of the heroic contained in the claims of veracity, even if the one chapter title to contain the word (II, vii – 'cette véritable histoire') is, perhaps predictably, among the greatest comic *tours de force* of the whole novel. As Muratore would have it, 'the truth of the tale depends less on establishing an illusion of reality than in reiterating the reality of the illusion' (*28*, p.106). There is then a repeated statement of indifference to the fictive reader's temperament in a chapter ending later on (II, ix), in the context of a widespread celebration currently being described in the hostelry, the spirit of which, by implication, is shared by the narrator and might, by extension, be hoped to infect the reader. As he skilfully creates the impression of gradually moving away from the scene described, so he effects as clearly as at any point in the novel the transition from narrator back to author persona (a process which is indicated in reverse on pp.182-83):

> Tandis que le bruit de tant de personnes, qui riaient ensemble, diminue peu à peu et se perd dans l'air, de la façon à peu près que fait la voix des échos, le chronologiste fidèle finira le présent chapitre sous le bon plaisir du lecteur bénévole ou malévole, ou tel que le ciel l'aura fait naître. (p.254)

Bringing these remarks together, we could see the subdivision in the fictive readership as between the 'lecteur bénévole', the reader who believes the story to be true (and thus makes of the 'chronologiste fidèle' a narrator) and the 'lecteur malévole', who does not believe its truth, thus making of him an author. As Waugh notes, 'the "Dear Reader" is no longer quite so passive and becomes in effect an acknowledged fully active player in a new conception of literature as a collective creation' (*33*, p.43).

All these impressions are then crucially endorsed by the episode of the mad priest, offering as it does the most extended earnest of authorial veracity in the novel. This cameo figure ('un prêtre du bas Maine, un peu fou mélancolique') effects in II, xvi a curious link between the author, the printer of the *Au Lecteur*, and the protagonists of a recent episode (such disorienting devices are thus deployed at later stages in the narrative, and not simply as opening shots). The mad priest reads during a visit to the printer the pages in which the episode was described and, since he knew those involved, points out the errors in the narration. This in turn leads the printer to express surprise, 'car il avait cru, comme beaucoup d'autres, que mon roman était un livre fait à plaisir' (p.308). The whole parenthesis thus allows the author persona to incorporate a claim of veracity into the primary fiction by way of the evidence of the (indisputably non-fictional) figure of the printer of the liminary text. The passage ends with the author persona expressing his

gratitude to the priest for the corrections he has allowed him to make
to the text (in exchange for advice given to the priest to resist the
publication of his 'livre plein de visions ridicules', p.309), thereby
affording empirical evidence of the author persona's sincerity. As a
result of this the plurality of motive which we see accorded to
various fictional participants is now extended to the fictive
readership: 'Quelqu'un m'accusera peut-être d'avoir conté ici une
particularité fort inutile, quelque autre m'en louera de beaucoup de
sincérité' (p.309). In either event, the audacity of this claim is only
reinforced by the fact that it is followed immediately by another of
the violent interruptions which punctuate the novel, inevitably
leading the empirical reader, according to his temperament, either to
conclude that the disingenuous author is nonetheless prone to
inventing for the sake of a good story or, more sympathetically, that
reality is just as chaotic and risible as fiction.

The narrator

If we shift now to relatively less foregrounded interventions, we
should first of all deal with those closest to the authorial persona,
afforded by the claims of veracity and non-omniscience, obvious
destabilizing devices in an apparently fictional and omniscient third-
person narrative. The degree of contemporary realism most of all
helps the narrator in his claims to be no more than a 'fidèle
historien'. We are meant to believe in the stories that he tells us
about his times, and indeed, with the exception of the elements of
exaggeration and coincidence, they are perfectly *vraisemblable*.
Their veracity is further reasserted by their purported continuation in
folk history: 'Le comédien Destin fit des prouesses à coups de poing,
dont l'on parle encore dans la ville du Mans' (p.70); 'j'ai su de
beaucoup de personnes qu'on ne l'avait [La Rancune] jamais vu rire'
(p.74); 'Le curé s'en retourna à Domfront sans aucune mauvaise
rencontre où, tant qu'il vivra, il contera son enlèvement' (p.136), a
feature that is then extended to the narrator himself, as he admits that
'je me suis souvent étonné depuis comment on avait pu faire par

hasard une si haute pyramide de viande sur si peu de base qu'est le cul d'une assiette' (p.250). Or, negatively:

> Quelque peine que j'aie prise à bien étudier La Rappinière, je n'ai jamais pu découvrir s'il était moins méchant envers Dieu qu'envers les hommes et moins injuste envers son prochain que vicieux en sa personne. Je sais seulement avec certitude que jamais homme n'a eu plus de vices ensemble et en plus éminent degré. (pp.301-2)

(Elsewhere the curé, ending his narration, notes of two combattants that '[ils] se battraient peut-être encore si on ne les avait séparés', p.239.) At the same time it is clear that he believes his function allows him not to have to attend to the particularities with which a true historian would concern himself. His contemporary world is offered to us as real, but not exhaustive: 'Quoiqu'un fidèle et exact historien soit obligé à particulariser les accidents importants de son histoire et les lieux où ils se sont passés, je ne vous dirai pas fort juste en quel endroit de notre hémisphère était la maisonnette où Ragotin mena ses confrères futurs' (p.304). Temporally, too, the narrative concentrates on extended close-ups of short periods of time; thus just as with its realism, so with its chronology, we are given a characteristic view of an actor's life by a selective and comic rather than a comprehensive or mimetic treatment. As Bénac comments, 'le trait de mœurs vrai sert de point de départ à la déformation burlesque ou à la satire et cela écarte Scarron de l'exact réalisme' (*2*, p.41).

The fact of the provincial setting is also indicative of a certain tone, and contributes further to the illusion of veracity; and those critics who are sceptical as to the contemporary detail contained in the novel should read the opening chapters of the *récit cadre* carefully. It is difficult to think of another work of fiction in the period in which the details of daily life in the French provinces are as generously scattered: language, meals, drink, sleeping habits, to say nothing of contemporary theatrical practice and literary taste. The description of a festive meal in I, xvi is especially complete, incorporating as it does the dishes served, the toasts drunk, and the etiquette at table (even if such details, which are so widespread in the primary 'historical' narrative, are disallowed in the secondary, *romanesque* one: 'Je ne vous dirai point exactement s'il avait soupé et s'il se coucha sans manger', p.90). The sheer ordinariness of life in the provinces is captured in the description of the dogs barking at night in a silent village (p.214), or the comings and goings at a hostelry in a small town, with a fire lit to warm the sheets, and a serving boy who arrives fresh from having cleaned a pair of boots (p.216). (As Bénac reminds us, 'depuis *Don Quichotte* et le roman picaresque, l'auberge était un décor international où se déroulait l'aventure', 2, p.41.) There is in addition a whole *dramatis personae* of minor figures, such as the niece of the curé de Domfront, his valets, the innkeepers and their wives and servants, the memorably grotesque couple of singers with inverted vocal parts who disrupt Le Destin's tale, an abbess and some nuns, not to mention the interventions of a goat, a brood of puppies, a greyhound, a mastiff, a ram and an anthropomorphic horse. More socially elevated provincial pastimes are recorded too in II, xvii, as the plays, hunts and balls initiated by the marquis d'Orsé are catalogued. Less flatteringly, the provinces are usually presented unfavourably in comparison with the capital: *provinciaux* are written off as 'la plus incommode nation du monde' (p.85), and their baser theatrical tastes implicitly despised: 'La farce divertit encore plus que la comédie, comme il arrive d'ordinaire partout ailleurs hors de Paris' (p.224); and a brief (explicit) digression on provincial speech and snobbery occurs in II, xvii, efficiently encapsulated in two conversational traits. Whereas in certain precursors the provincial setting is purely accidental, for Scarron the provinciality of the actors is an essential part of their identity; and that identity is placed in turn by the narrator at the service of his claims of veracity.

Claims of non-omniscience abound too, and, together with other similar devices, continue right through the text, rather than simply being established at the outset. Recalling the episode of a horse ridden by Ragotin (itself the subject of an authorial intervention), we read that 'Le Destin monta sur un cheval, sur lequel Ragotin venait d'arriver du Mans' but are then parenthetically reminded '(je ne sais pas au vrai si c'était le même qui l'avait déjà jeté par terre)' (p.206). Again in II, xiii, the non-omniscience interrupts the syntax to such a degree that it has to be restored:

> Enfin les deux jeunes amants se rassurèrent et s'étant dit quelques douces tendresses (car il y avait lieu d'en dire après ce qui venait d'arriver, et pour moi, je n'en doute point, quoique je n'en sache rien de particulier); après donc s'être bien attendri le cœur l'un à l'autre [...] (p.268)

Non-omniscience may elsewhere occur in a progression, leading to bathos, such as when the narrator concludes a sequence: 'La Rappinière en devint tout violet, sa femme en rougit, le valet en jura, La Caverne en sourit, La Rancune n'y prit peut-être pas garde et, pour Destin, je n'ai pas bien su l'effet que cela fit sur son esprit' (p.72); or, more simply, afford a brief comic parenthesis: '[...] cette province abonde en personnes ventrues. Je laisse aux naturalistes le soin d'en chercher la raison aussi bien que de la graisse des chapons du pays' (p.236). Such examples coexist (more rarely) with a narratorial assertion of omniscience, such as when the facts of La Rappinière's account of an episode are corrected: 'il est bien vrai qu'il rendit la boîte, comme il avait promis; mais il n'était pas vrai qu'elle fût au Mans puisqu'il l'avait sur lui à l'heure même' (p.303), although, ironically enough, both features serve to establish the same claims.

A related variant is the presentation of motivation as ambiguous: 'La Rappinière [...] demeura comme immobile, ou d'admiration, ou parce qu'il n'était pas encore assez en colère' (p.70); 'Le frère du mort fit semblant d'être triste ou le fut véritablement' (p.237 – or elsewhere, with the ordering of probability reversed, in 'se trouvant un peu fatiguée ou feignant de l'être, p.255); 'Le Destin et Léandre ne s'émurent pas beaucoup du conte que le curé leur donnait pour bon, soit qu'ils ne le trouvassent pas si plaisant qu'il leur avait dit, ou qu'ils ne fussent pas alors en humeur de rire' (p.238); or taking the form of a *correctio*: 'une compagnie de Bohémiens [...] s'y étaient arrêtés sous prétexte que la femme du capitaine avait été pressée d'accoucher *ou plutôt* par la facilité que ces voleurs espérèrent de trouver à manger impunément des volailles d'une métairie écartée du grand chemin' (p.304, my emphasis). This finds its most sustained expression at the end of the first part, in which the interpretation of motive is delegated to the characters who witness the episode (of Roquebrune choosing to stay with the actresses to avoid one of the story's many violent disruptions, rather than following the men who go after the thieves): 'Quelques-uns ont cru que c'était par poltronnerie et d'autres, plus indulgents, ont trouvé qu'il n'avait pas mal fait de demeurer auprès des dames' (p.206).

A further vital function fulfilled by the narrator consists in the explicit transposition of the interpolated stories, whose previous fictional identity is fully acknowledged, into his own narrative mode, whoever they are in fact supposed to be narrated by. Thus the primary narrator makes it quite clear that when a Spanish woman is speaking, no attempt will be made to imitate her defective French; and the same is true of Ragotin: 'Vous allez voir cette histoire dans le suivant chapitre, non telle que la conta Ragotin, mais comme je la pourrai conter d'après un des auditeurs qui me l'a apprise. Ce n'est donc pas Ragotin qui parle, c'est moi' (p.86). A further advantage of this device is evident from the facility with which narratorial interventions may occur within the interpolated stories, just as at the primary narrative level. Offering a subtle variant on this, we also note on occasion the use of 'style indirect libre': 'Le Destin eût bien voulu dîner en liberté avec ses camarades, mais *comment eût-il refusé sa très humble servante madame Bouvillon*, qui l'envoya quérir pour dîner aussitôt que l'on eut servi' (p.255); or 'le capitaine bohême le [Ragotin] fit enrager à force de lui parler civilement et fut assez effronté pour le louer de sa bonne mine *qui sentait son homme de qualité et qui ne le faisait pas peu repentir d'être entré par ignorance dans son château*' (p.304, my emphases).

Finally, asides are consistently deployed for a number of functions. They may indicate selectivity: 'j'en pourrais dire cent choses rares, que je laisse de peur d'être trop long' (p.72); glossing, or rather failing to gloss a term (here '*non plus ultra*'): 'Ceux qui n'entendront pas ces trois petits mots latins [...] se les feront expliquer s'il leur plaît' (p.112); or may introduce or abandon digressions (e.g. p.250). Elsewhere we find examples indicating authenticity by the recurrent use of 'peut-être' (e.g. p.70), vagueness, with the equally simple 'si je m'en souviens' (e.g. p.69) or reinforcement (here explicitly parenthetical): 'Sa mauvaise intention la faisant rougir (car elles rougissent aussi, les dévergondées)' (p.257); introducing illustrative simile: 'comme on fait quand on veut amasser quelque chose qui est à terre' (p.79) or irony, such as when two capuchins become involved in a fight 'par charité' (p.70); or conveying an informal impression of orality: 'madame sa mère, j'entends du marié' leading to 'madame Bouvillon (c'est ainsi que s'appelait la mère du marié)' (p.249). At certain points whole successions of such interventions occur, as in the opening of I, xiv, appropriately enhancing the high comedy of the scene. The narrator is also present in a more obtrusive way by the occasional insertion of a *sententia*. Thus of Le Destin's advice to Léandre, delivered in the knowledge that 'les personnes qui aiment ne sont pas capables de croire d'autres conseils que ceux de leur passion et sont plus à plaindre qu'à blâmer' (p.234); or, of Ragotin: 'En vérité, quand la fortune a commencé de persécuter un misérable, elle le persécute toujours' (p.316).

We might in conclusion reassemble our persona, and consider his attitude towards the ordinary ways of the world, tainted as they are with the acerbity that was to characterize certain contemporary and later *moralistes*, yet without any of their apparent pessimism:

Dans toutes les villes subalternes du royaume, il y a d'ordinaire un tripot où s'assemblent tous les jours les fainéants de la ville, les uns pour jouer, les autres pour regarder ceux qui jouent; c'est là que l'on [...] épargne

> fort peu le prochain et que les absents sont assassinés à
> coups de langue. (p.69)

An attitude of disillusioned tolerance is evinced towards the foibles
of the characters he invents or records, redolent of Boileau's fourth
Satire in its identification of the universality of madness: 'Tous les
hommes sont fous et, malgré tous leurs soins / Ne diffèrent entre eux
que du plus ou du moins' (*8*, p.36) :

> Sache le sot qui s'en scandalise que tout homme est sot
> en ce bas monde, aussi bien que menteur, les uns plus et
> les autres moins; et moi qui vous parle, peut-être plus sot
> que les autres, quoique j'aie plus de franchise à l'avouer
> et que mon livre n'étant qu'un ramas de sottises, j'espère
> que chaque sot y trouvera un petit caractère de ce qu'il
> est ... (p.87)

Vitally, however, the author persona and his book are here
incorporated into the universal state, together with the fictive reader.
In this way he establishes a further *rapport* with this reader in their
shared capacity not to be exempt from folly, but to recognize and, in
the end, to celebrate it: 'Scarron fonde l'école des romanciers qui
connaissent les adresses du métier, mais qui en font les lecteurs
complices', and is thus able to 'rallier la sympathie de tous ses
lecteurs qui s'accordent à louer sa gaîté' (*20*, p.203). The prevalent
spirit of the troupe contributes as well to a sense of wit and good
humour, characterized as it is by teasing, *badinage* and word play,
qualities shared by the whole spectrum of its members (see for
example the dialogue in I, xvi, pp.162-64, or the passage of repartee
between Roquebrune and La Rancune in I, xix, p.180). Even Ragotin
is capable of turning a disaster into a farce, as we see after he has
been released from his chamber pot in II, ix: 'Enfin il s'en tira mieux
qu'on ne pensait et se mit à chanter de toute sa force les premières
chansons qui lui vinrent à la bouche, ce qui changea le grand bruit de
voix confuses en de grands éclats de risées' (p.254). Appropriately,
therefore, laughter is more often than not the end point of scenes of

disorder, and at the dénouement of the (visually brilliant) meal episode in II, viii, the narrator simply concludes: 'Enfin on acheva de rire, parce que l'on ne peut pas rire toujours' (p.251). Place, conviviality and acting all come together (albeit briefly) as the first part ends: 'On soupa à la mode du Mans, c'est-à-dire que l'on fit fort bonne chère, et tout le monde prit place pour entendre la comédie' (p.205). If the work has a moral, therefore, it must lie in the tolerance of the absurdity of the human condition as, through the vicissitudes of the story, a certain good humour prevails, in a spirit not dissimilar to Rabelais's definition of *pantagruélisme*: 'Certaine gayeté d'esprit conficte en mespris des choses fortuites' (*13*, p.11-12). Coulet, as so often, magisterially resumes Scarron's qualities: 'Il n'a pas l'optimisme conquérant qui fertilise l'imagination de Rabelais, mais il est inspiré par un désir de joie qui lui fait renforcer et multiplier les occasions de rire. [...] Scarron n'a pas besoin de l'analyse psychologique pour être bon moraliste, le rire est en lui-même compréhension et jugement' (*20*, pp.203-04).

7. Towards a Definition

Baroque and classicism

It is tempting to see the *Roman comique* as showing certain features which are commonly attributed to a baroque aesthetic; and, albeit more speculatively, to identify aspects of it which correspond to a possible definition of classicism. It should however straightaway be recognized that the same features of the text may attract a different description according to the perspective and the distance adopted, and thus to identify the high degree of subjectivity and imprecision in any such labels.

Thematically, the features of the troupe of travelling players, which we considered at the outset of this study, recall features which have attracted the epithet 'baroque'. Rousset, for example, evokes as a component of the term 'l'unité mouvante d'un ensemble multiforme en voie de métamorphose' (*31*, p.181), and encapsulates thereby two critical features of the novel's composite hero: mobility and metamorphosis. The protean is not just limited to the quality of the troupe, however, and different characters take on different identities within and beyond their theatrical vocation at various points in the story. In addition, the theatricality of the stage is mirrored, as we have seen, in the theatrical portrayal of the actors' world.

Such a description could furthermore be applied to the work as a whole on a structural and aesthetic level, shifting as it is in genre and perspectives, and offering, in one reading at least, an evolution in emphasis within the two extant books 'du burlesque vers le romanesque' (*32*, p.466). Alongside this, we have noted the presence of asymmetries, mirrorings and illusions, together with exuberance and 'délire verbal' (*19*, p.167), and, finally, 'la soumission de la fonction au décor' (*31*, p.182), here exemplified *par excellence* by the privileging of the form of narration through the interventionist and ironizing author persona / narrator. Chédozeau, whilst recognizing the inadequacy of the term within the domain of the novel, nonetheless finds the best definition to unite these features, when he identifies a 'baroque ludique' (*19*, p.167).

Equally, I have already implicitly indicated certain of the more important classical features: the selective concealment of artifice; the relative decorum, notably in the interpolated and retrospective stories; finally the concern to ensure a careful admixture of the strands of the text, so that, vitally, a balance is achieved. Just a look at the chapter headings will show how the narrative devices, although often outrageous *per se*, are never exploited over an excessively long period. As the author persona implicitly recognizes in an aside in I, viii: 'Il y a bien d'autres choses à dire sur ce sujet; mais il faut les ménager et les placer en divers endroits de mon livre pour diversifier' (p.85). Thus relief is a constituent feature in the sequence of chapters; just as the lighter tone of *badinage* and frivolity is welcome after the density of event of the interpolated stories, so does their consequential narrative provide in turn some relief from the disorder and interruptions of the primary level. Scarron 'sait doser ses effets' (*32*, p.515) and, as a result, we may discern the paradoxical achievement of consistency of instability.

In this light, and despite its superficial heterogeneity, there is a real unity in Scarron's writing, even if it requires a degree of detachment from the text to recognize it; and that unity lies in the progressive establishment and exploitation of three features. First in providing a communal ethos, uniting the troupe with its additional members, promoting a spirit of 'bonne chère', and maintaining a kind of stoic good humour through the wildest vicissitudes of fortune, current or past. The exemplary figure of Le Destin takes these qualities furthest, to the point at which they encounter the characteristic virtues of *honnêteté*. This is a moral unity. Secondly, it lies in a fictional pact between author persona and *lecteur bénévole*, mirrored in the secondary narrators and their hearers in a community of attentive listeners and entertaining *raconteurs*. All these elements in turn show us, the empirical readers, how to derive a salutary, even therapeutic enjoyment from our receptive approach to the complex totality of the novel. This is a narrative unity. Finally, and most important of all, it is achieved by what I have labelled the 'texture' of the writing, a quality which is exemplified when narratorial features from the primary text, such as shifts of register and puncturing techniques, are incorporated in the secondary narratives; or, complementarily to this, when adventures and sentiment are prioritized on the primary narrative level in the world of the actors. This is a tonal unity.

The modesty *topoi* of his unassuming and sympathetic persona should not allow us to underestimate the skill of the author of the *Roman comique*. All the features we have considered contribute to the character of this incomplete work which, despite its apparent disorder and extensive attention to low-life, despite its parody and realism, comes across to us paradoxically as a work of proportion and taste: Scarron '[n'est] jamais vulgaire même dans la grossièreté ni méchant dans la caricature' (*20*, p.203). In this concern for unity within a balanced framework of relative decorum and *honnêteté*, the *Roman comique* may be thought to come close to some ideal of classicism.

It might therefore be appropriate to proceed by mentioning those features of this novel that remind us that *La Princesse de Clèves* is soon to be written (in 1678), and thus point to commonplaces within narrative fiction of the period as a genre. On several occasions, predominantly within the interpolated stories of the *Roman comique*, we find incidents or phrases which are shared with the later work, and although there may be no more to say than that these are coincidences, the chronological proximity makes likely some element of a shared *topos*. The role of imagination in 'affaires du cœur' reminds us for example of Mme de Clèves's 'devoir imaginaire': 'Je vois bien que je quitte la plus belle personne du monde pour une autre qui ne l'est peut-être que dans mon imagination' (p.97); the theme of *repos*: 'S'il trompe ce bon curé pour me tromper, ajouta-t-elle, s'il n'a pas dessein de m'épouser comme il me le veut faire accroire, quelles violences ne dois-je pas craindre d'un homme tout à fait esclave de ses passions' – together with the fears about marrying: 'quelle misère dans le monde approchera de la mienne quand sa fantaisie sera passée?' (p.227); the idea of immediate mutual recognition of lovers (such as at the ball): 'Ils furent ensemble le reste du jour et se plurent tellement l'un à l'autre que [...]' (p.188); even the *aveu*, albeit a comic one (p.108). On a more physical note, we identify the role played by an object, here a casket with a portrait, in a love intrigue (p.303), or of livery colour (p.88) or absence from a ball (p.92) in the interpretation of feelings – the latter both features of Ragotin's first intercalated story (I, ix). Such glimpses go some way towards showing how, although there are many disparate features between novels in the period, there are also some intertextual conventions in common between even the most unlikely examples; and, significantly, how such parallels point to the adaptations of the *novelas cortas* as the sub-genre whose potential for development in a more restrained mode was the most fertile.

And yet if we look more closely at some details of the text, first of all in the chapter where matters of literary aesthetics are explicitly discussed, any such kind of security breaks down. Theoretically, it is stressed, the subjects of novels cannot be made into classical theatre, as Ragotin would wish, 'sans beaucoup de fautes contre la bienséance et contre le jugement' (p.105); and the 'jeune conseiller de Rennes' embarks on a whole anti-classical outburst, proposing that

> ...les sujets connus, dont on pouvait faire des pièces régulières, avaient tous été mis en œuvre; que l'histoire était épuisée et que l'on serait réduit à la fin à se dispenser de la règle des vingt-quatre heures; que le peuple et la plus grande partie du monde ne savaient point à quoi étaient bonnes les règles sévères du théâtre; [et] que l'on prenait plus de plaisir à voir représenter les choses qu'à ouïr des récits... (p.184)

Empirically too, the restrained register is persistently disrupted: both retrospective narrations and performances of great plays are interrupted by falling asleep, brawls and drunken interventions. Even more ironically, the apologia for the theatre, where the author persona reassures the reader that 'la comédie [...] est aujourd'hui purgée [...] de tout ce qu'elle avait de licencieux' and 'la farce est comme abolie' is immediately followed by the appearance of Madame Bouvillon '[qui] portait d'ordinaire sur elle, bon an mal an, trente quintaux de chair' (p.249), and by the scene in which 'la jeune mariée, [...] s'ébouffant de rire en commençant de boire [...], couvrit le visage de sa belle-mère et celui de son mari de la plus grande partie de ce qui était dans son verre et distribua le reste sur la table et sur les habits de ceux qui y étaient assis' (p.250). In addition, the provision of the author persona and his relationship to the fictive reader is a long way from any kind of classical model: the 'lecteur bénévole ou malévole' is too close a descendant of the 'beuveurs [et] verolez' of Rabelais; and the very fact of an intrusive, ironic voice is itself destructive of the impassivity of much classical discourse.

We thus feel that a classical discourse *is* available, in the retrospective narratives, Spanish stories (especially the later ones) and dramatic performances; and, even within the primary text, impeccable ternary rhythms occur at moments of high comic disorder (p.237). It is admitted as one narrative possibility, but is persistently negated or postponed in favour of a polyvocal alternative. As DeJean remarks, 'the reader finds himself in a world in which classical tradition and style have been physically deformed' (*39*, p.27), and the writing is just as often (deliberately we have therefore to conclude) jagged and asymmetrically ordered. It is as if Scarron perpetually builds bridges between exuberance and decorum, only to break them down again, resulting overall in the paradoxical impression of '[la] cohérence profonde d'un récit en apparence incohérent' (*20*, p.207).

Le roman pur

I want secondly to suggest a further set of novelistic criteria which may, surprisingly, give us some terms, not with which to describe features of the *Roman comique*, nor its relationship to contemporary writing and aesthetics, but to discern the nature of it as a phenomenon. These are the terms introduced by André Gide in his attempt to define the ideal of the 'roman pur', a conflation of the anti-novel and the elusive yet endlessly desirable novelistic ideal, exemplified by the activities both of Gide himself and of the fictional writer of a novel entitled *Les Faux-Monnayeurs* (Edouard) within the work of the same name.

i) 'Le grand défaut [...], c'est de couper sa tranche [de vie] toujours dans le même sens; dans le sens du temps, en longueur. Pourquoi pas en largeur? ou en profondeur?' (*10*, p.1081).

The *Roman comique* militates against just such a horizontal axis in its mode of narration. The story evolves retrospectively and / or non-sequentially in the general and the particular. Most globally, as the narrating personae increase, digressions (and digressions within digressions) impede any impetus for contemporary event, forward movement or resolution. Certain chapters are virtually static, and simply depend on one or two comic episodes (such as I, xx – in this case the episodes are furthermore parallel); others are entirely self-contained (such as the Spanish *nouvelles*); and others again (I, xv, for example) constitute a microcosm of the complex structure of the work as a whole. And within individual chapters, interruptions and asides abound, together with shifts of register and subject-matter. In all these ways, in the totality as in the detail of the work, the slow progressive chronology ('longueur') is more often than not overpowered by the dominant regressive ('largeur') or static ('profondeur') axes.

What replaces the horizontal thrust is a narrative mode which broadens and deepens the reader's picture. The two strands of retrogression expand the primary narration and characterizations, as well as affording an extension of the fictional world that is at once chronological, geographical and social. Further, the interplay of the different strands of the novel, by frustrating any desire to proceed rapidly towards a conclusion, promotes a non-progressive reading pleasure. We might indeed wonder what the ideal reading span is, given the occasionally emphatic links made between chapters ('Il vous souviendra, s'il vous plaît, que dans le précédent chapitre [...]', p.137); but if we are held back from a plot-driven reading by all manner of devices it is in order the better to appreciate the texture of the writing, its depth, at any given stage in the reading experience.

ii) 'Ne jamais profiter de l'élan acquis – telle est la règle de mon jeu' (*11*, pp.69-70).

The *Roman comique* is a novel about interruption. We find interrupted narrations, or ones in which the hearer falls asleep; as early as the second chapter, a conversation is resumed by La Rappinière 'que les coups de poing avaient interrompue' (p.67); and certain chapters are effectively one long interruption, such as II, vi, with the fight episode encasing the death of the host, and the whole appropriately ending on an authorial *sententia*. Elsewhere a new chapter will have to regain the narrative momentum, after a previous one has reached apparent stasis or closure, thus I, xxi (p.184). Even more fundamentally, we note the sense of a new start given by the opening of the second part, reflecting, albeit more briefly, that of the first. And the interrupted journeyings serve as a spatial metaphor for the narrative discontinuity.

The theme of the interrupted performance of a play, as well, is one that recurs frequently in the work as a whole, and indeed it is on such an event that it comes to an end. Time and again, productions are thwarted, and no sooner is a performance begun or discussed than the attention of the reader is directed away from it, for example by what is happening in the audience. In II, xvii, the narrator begins with the description of a production (p.314), but thereafter no more is said about the play, and the remainder of the chapter contains a highly comic description of a fight breaking out in the audience because Ragotin is sitting behind someone who is bigger than he is. Most ironically of all, the great interrupters, Ragotin and La Rancune, interrupt themselves in turn: 'Un verre de vin bu de part et d'autre interrompit quelque temps la conversation' (p.109); and the very last chapter appropriately carries the title: 'De quelle façon le sommeil de Ragotin fut interrompu' (p.342).

Finally, we have little or no impression of the *récit cadre* having any significant sense of impetus towards a resolution. The major features have all been introduced by the end of the first part; and the second does little more than develop and diversify a pre-established model. The incompleteness of the *Roman comique* is not just contingent, therefore, it is definitional. The 'nonteleological' writing and the deliberate tone of unfinality with which it ends (irrespective of any putative third book) all point to the business of completion as an irrelevance; and, just as strongly, they designate an endless fertility in the strands of narrative, which are nourished in turn by the *récit cadre*. '"Pourrait être continué..." c'est sur ces mots que je voudrais terminer' (*10*, p.1201).

iii) 'La *pureté*, en art comme partout, c'est cela qui importe' (*11*, p.59).

The elusive definition of purity can be deemed to entail three dominant characteristics of the *Roman comique*. It is first of all pure – that is uncontaminated by ideological engagement – in its refusal to address metaphysical, political or moral issues. Putting it at its most absolute, there is 'nothing beyond literature, nothing indeed beyond style' (*39*, p.47), and in fact the paucity of the primary plot may on occasion make the question of the novel's subject seem redundant or at best peripheral. It is secondly pure – that is concerned with art for its own sake – in its entirely self-sufficient and brilliantly comic developments of ludic episodes. 'La poétique du burlesque est caractérisée principalement par une écriture auto-référentielle qui met de façon décisive le langage au premier plan' (*21*, p.331); and here Scarron does uniquely, in one possible understanding of Mallarmé's* celebrated formula, contrive to 'donner un sens plus pur aux mots de la tribu' ('Le Tombeau d'Edgar Poe' in *12*, p.189). Most of all it is pure because it is self-reflexive and self-justificatory; and the composition and status of the novel are in one reading the principal subjects of the *Roman comique*. As we have seen, there is a gradual emergence of a convincing *romanesque*; but also a diffuse set of reflections on the theatrical and the novelistic nature of life; on the areas of overlap between these two modes of stylization; and on the truthfulness of fiction. And just as it is self-conscious in the business of drawing attention to the mechanics of its own composition, so is it self-justificatory in the defence of its own genre and existence.

But of course, 'ce pur roman, il ne parviendra jamais à l'écrire' (*11*, p.59). The final component of novelistic purity is non-existence, since the novel, for which Gide's creation Edouard borrows the English epithet 'lawless', is incapable of that absolute purity to which more rigorously defined genres, such as the sonnet or the fugue, may more closely approximate. The subjectless novel is unwritable in a semantic medium, and the ultimate impurity of our novel lies in the contradiction of the title. On the one hand, it is the author's single example of the genre, it is 'le' *Roman comique*, and Scarron, like Gide, resisted the term *roman* for his other prose writings (and, already in the prefatory material, refers to 'mon roman, mon livre'). Yet at the same time he has not succeeded, any more than will Gide, in the aim to 'purger le roman de tous les éléments qui n'appartiennent pas spécifiquement au roman' (*11*, p.57), as the theatrical subject-matter, style and indeed apologia amply demonstrate.

Conclusion

The whole novel can thus only be resumed as a web of contradictions, since each time we feel we have found a dominant characteristic, it is quickly thrown into question. Scarron's novel is a complex work, and a tightly woven work. It treats of actors, provinces, adventures, travels and taverns; but also of the theatre, the novel and aesthetics. Further, these subjects do not exist in isolation, but interconnect in a variety of ways. If we return finally to Serroy, we may perhaps see in his juxtaposition of antonyms the only logical way to deal with such a degree of diversity. He suggests the *Roman comique* be read in a binary framework, since 'il tire toutes les conséquences de ce principe de dualité'; and so combines such epithets as 'satirique et sentimental, burlesque et héroïque, réaliste et romanesque' (*32*, p.446). To these we might add other terms, such as baroque and classical, diffuse and controlled, unified and fragmented, disillusioned and optimistic and, bringing them all together, pure and impure.

In the end, the *Roman comique* is itself, it is *sui generis*, and shares with Corneille's similarly entitled *Illusion comique* the quality of 'un étrange monstre' (*9*, p.193). It may serve as an illustration of contemporary aesthetic terms such as *burlesque* or *anti-roman*; or subsequently imposed labels such as baroque or metafiction; or indeed fit fairly neatly into parallels with Rabelais, Diderot or Gide. But what we must above all retain is the fact that the majority of such views follow and do not precede the text. They allow us to talk about it by helping us to realize how a work which, by its fertility, elicited from succeeding generations of novelists a proliferation of successors, has equally provoked succeeding generations of interpreters to a similar (or greater) extent in their attempts to describe and account for it. Its fertility is at once fictional and critical. It is the fertility of a unique work of art.

Appendix I: Continuations, Endings and Translations

Le Roman comique: troisième partie appeared in 1663, published anonymously 'chez A. Offray' in Lyons. There is some slender documentary evidence concerning Scarron's intentions regarding a third book, and Serroy in particular stresses that the extant books encourage the reader to envisage such a continuation. He suggests that 'l'analyse des pistes tracées par Scarron laisse clairement apparaître que Le Destin [...] est, en réalité, le fils du comte de Glaris. De même, il est probable que L'Etoile est [...] fille de condition', and therefore that 'on peut raisonnablement penser que la reconnaissance finale des deux couples de comédiens, et [...] le mariage qui en eût marqué le couronnement, auraient formé le canevas de cette troisième partie', even if 'pour le reste toutes les hypothèses restent possibles' (5, pp.341-42). The *Suite d'Offray* in fact resists the first of these developments, although it does propose marriages between both Le Destin and L'Etoile and Léandre and Angélique. The emphasis is however firmly on Ragotin, now admitted to the troupe of actors, and whose death in a drowning accident (after several aborted attempts at suicide following the marriage of L'Etoile), concludes the work. The majority of the episodes takes place at Alençon, where the troupe has moved on to, and a number of minor stylistic features of the original are retained. In particular, there are interpolated stories (two indeed follow each other in the closing chapters), most notably the 'Histoire du Prieur de Saint-Louis', a long *romanesque* intervention, drawn however neither from a member of the troupe nor from an independent Spanish tradition but from the adventures, disappointment in love, and finally ordination of a newly invented tangential figure. The basic direction here, however maladroitly handled, is thus towards a resolution, in accordance with De Armas's reading, for whom

'Scarron's main concern is the final harmony which he already mirrored in the last interpolated story' (*36*, p.91).

La Suite du Roman comique by the prolific novelist Jean de Préchac followed in 1679. The emphasis now falls on to the couple of Inézille and the 'opérateur', who are made into the principal sources of invention, in the former case as a narrator and in the latter by the introduction of the powers of magic. In other respects, we find the same imitative features, with an interesting updating of context afforded by the performance of Racine's tragedy *Bérénice*, premièred in 1670. Here, however, we are dealing not with a completion but with a continuation, in accordance with a more open-ended view of the original as a source of further developments, rather than as an incomplete entity awaiting ultimate fictional resolution. In this respect, therefore, it is 'plus proche de l'esprit de Scarron' (*5*, p.366). It nonetheless attracted such a resolution, provided by Louis Barre in 1858. Finally, the *Suite et conclusion du Roman comique par M. D. L.* finished the story, in both senses, in 1771. This version strays furthest of all from the tone of the original, however, and sacrifices its comic tone for an exclusively *romanesque* emphasis, effected by a foregrounding of the figure of Le Destin. In addition, there were transpositions into other genres, in the form of a dramatization by Champmeslé and La Fontaine, *Ragotin ou le roman comique*, in 1684; and a *Roman comique mis en vers* by Le Tellier d'Orvilliers (1773).

It remains to mention the two eighteenth-century translations into English: the very close rendering by Tom Brown, John Savage and others (*The whole comical works of Monsieur Scarron*, London, S. and J. Sprint, 1700), adorned in the 1892 edition (London, Lawrence and Bullen, 2 vols) by the engravings of J.-B. Oudry, and recently reprinted in a modern critical edition (*46*); and the much freer adaptation by Oliver Goldsmith (*The comic romance of Monsieur Scarron*, London, W. Griffin, 1775).

Appendix II: Literary and Historical References

Ariosto, Ludovico (1444-1533): Italian Renaissance poet, whose heroï-comic masterpiece *Orlando Furioso* (1516, 1532) deals with the legendary hero of Carolingian France, Roland.

Aristotle (384 BC-322 BC): Ancient Greek writer, perceived in seventeenth-century France as the authoritative aesthetic theoretician, notably in the regular composition of dramatic works.

Beys, Charles (c. 1610-59): minor poet and dramatist, whose best-known play is *L'Hôpital des fous* (1634).

Boccaccio, Giovanni (1313-75): Italian Renaissance writer, best known for his racy collection of short stories, the *Decameron* (1350-53). His major French imitator was Marguerite de Navarre.

Boileau(-Despréaux), Nicolas (1636-1711): classical theoretician and satirist. In addition to his *Art poétique* (1674) his best-known works are his *Satires* (1660-67) and *Epîtres* (1669-95).

Cervantes, Miguel de (1547-1616): Spanish novelist, whose masterpiece, *Don Quijote* (1605, 1615), and briefer *Novelas ejemplares* (1613) exerted a formative influence on French narrative fiction in the early seventeenth century.

Corneille, Pierre (1606-84): dramatist and dramatic theoretician, whose long career is usually considered to have reached its high point in the years 1636-44 with *L'Illusion comique* (1636), *Le Cid* (1636), *Horace* (1640), *Cinna* (1641), *Polyeucte* (1642) and *Rodogune* (1644). *Nicomède* dates from 1651.

Descartes, René (1596-1650): philosopher, whose *Discours de la méthode* (1637) and *Méditations métaphysiques* (1647) insisted on the primacy of reason in metaphysical and physical knowledge.

Des Périers, Bonaventure (1510-44): Renaissance *conteur*, in whose posthumous *Nouvelles récréations* (1558) certain self-conscious narrative devices are encountered.

Diderot, Denis (1713-84): novelist and *philosophe*, whose posthumous experimental novel *Jacques le fataliste* (1796) appears in many respects to be a descendant of *Le Roman comique*.

Foucquet, Marie-Madeleine de Castille-Villemareuil, madame (1633-1716): wife of the Surintendant des Finances, Nicolas Foucquet, who was to be disgraced in 1661. The dedication of the second part of the novel to her would suggest that Scarron had enjoyed her patronage (see *3*, p.429, n. 85).

Furetière, Antoine (1619-88): lexicographer and comic novelist, whose *Roman bourgeois* (1666) comes closest in the period to the status of an anti-novel.

Garnier, Robert (1544-90): dramatist, whose somewhat static plays, on classical and Biblical subjects, characterized tragedy in the period before the *Roman comique*. The tragi-comedy *Bradamante* dates from 1582.

Gide, André (1869-1951): novelist and theoretician of the novel, whose *roman pur*, *Les Faux-Monnayeurs* and its accompanying *Journal des Faux-Monnayeurs* (both 1926) may be seen as distant descendants of the *Roman comique*.

Gomberville, Marin le Roy de (1600-74): heroic novelist, known above all for his exotic *Polexandre* (1619-37).

Hardy, Alexandre (1570-1632): tragic dramatist, whose vast output dominated the period immediately before the *Roman comique*.

La Bruyère, Jean de (1645-96): *moraliste*, whose single work, *Les Caractères* (1688-94), affords a wittily disenchanted view of the later seventeenth century.

La Calprenède, Gautier de Costes de (1610-63): heroic novelist, whose massive works included *Cassandre* (1642-45) and *Cléopâtre* (1646-57), and who reached a peak of popularity in the 1640s.

La Fayette, Marie-Madeleine Pioche de la Vergne, comtesse de (1634-93): novelist, credited with the first example of a classical, as of a modern psychological novel, *La Princesse de Clèves* (1678).

La Rochefoucauld, François, duc de (1613-80): *moraliste*, whose acerbic *Maximes* (1665) encapsulate the wit and cynicism of the *salons*, as well as defining the ideal of *honnêteté*.

Lazarillo de Tormes (anonymous; circa 1554): the first Spanish picaresque novel, translated into French in 1561.

L'Hermite, (François) Tristan (1601-65): *libertin* poet, novelist and dramatist, whose most successful play was the tragedy *La Marianne* (1636).

Malherbe, François de (1555-1628): poet and poetic theorist, credited with inaugurating the refinement and impassivity of the French language as it was to be manifested later in the seventeenth century.

Mallarmé, Stéphane (1842-98): symbolist poet, exponent of the doctrine of 'la poésie pure'.

Marguerite de Navarre, (1492-1549): *conteur* and imitator of Boccaccio, whose incomplete *Heptaméron* (1559) juxtaposes brief stories with theological or moralizing deliberations.

Molière (Jean-Baptiste Poquelin) (1622-73): comic dramatist, whose large output included *L'Ecole des femmes* (1662), *Le Tartuffe* (1664), *Dom Juan* (1665), *Le Misanthrope* (1666), *Le Bourgeois Gentilhomme* (1670) and *Le Malade imaginaire* (1673), certain of whose dominant themes and techniques are anticipated in the *Roman comique*.

Nouveau roman (Le): literary movement of the mid-twentieth century, whose creative writing was grounded in theory, and which sought to renew the novel by the achievement of a greater realism.

Pascal, Blaise (1623-62): religious and scientific writer, whose best-known works are the polemical *Lettres provinciales* (1656-57) and the unfinished apology for the Christian religion known as the *Pensées* (1670).

Plutarch (AD 46/9-AD 125): Ancient Greek writer of the didactic biographies of great men, the *Lives*.

Rabelais, François (1494-1553): Renaissance writer of the (unfinished) *chroniques* of the giants Gargantua and Pantagruel. This comic masterpiece, published between 1532 and 1564, is above all characterized by extreme erudition alongside or within verbal exuberance and scatological excess.

Racine, Jean (1639-99): tragic dramatist, widely considered to represent the apogee of neo-classical tragedy in such works as *Andromaque* (1667), *Britannicus* (1669), *Bérénice* (1670) and *Phèdre* (1677).

Retz, Paul de Gondi, cardinal de (1613-79): cleric, rebel and memoir-writer, with whom Scarron sided during the civil wars known as the Fronde (1648-53), and to whom, in his capacity as coadjutor to the Archbishop of Paris, the first book of the *Roman comique* is dedicated.

Rojas Villandrando, Agustín de (1577-?): Spanish playwright and novelist, whose *Viaje entretenido* (1603) bears certain superficial similarities to *Le Roman comique*.

Rotrou, Jean (1609-50): prolific tragic and comic dramatist, often associated with the term 'baroque', whose best-known play is *Le Véritable saint Genest* (1645).

Saint-Amant, Marc-Antoine de Gérard, sieur de (1594-1661): versatile poet, friend of Théophile de Viau, and founder member of the Académie Française.

Scudéry, Madeleine de (1607-1701): heroic novelist, whose monumental works *Le Grand Cyrus* (1649-53) and *Clélie* (1654-60) are periodically evoked in the *Roman comique*.

Sévigné, Marie de Rabutin-Chantal, marquise de (1626-96): letter-writer, whose extensive correspondence, notably with her daughter, raises the previously informal genre to new literary heights.

Sorel, Charles (1600-74): novelist and bibliographer, whose *Histoire comique de Francion* (1623-33) shares certain features with the *Roman comique*, whilst retaining others which link it to writers of the previous century.

Urfé, Honoré d' (1567-1625): novelist, creator of the great pastoral *L'Astrée* (1607-27).

Viau, Théophile de (1590-1626): poet and dramatist, associated with the *libertin* movement, whose best-known play is the tragedy *Pyrame et Thisbé* (1623).

Selected Bibliography

EDITIONS

Recommended editions of the *Roman comique* and of contemporary comic prose texts are as follows:
1. *Romanciers du XVIIe siècle*, ed. A. Adam, Paris, Gallimard (Bibliothèque de la Pléiade), 1958. Brings together Sorel, Scarron, Furetière and La Fayette. Original spelling and useful introduction.
2. Scarron, Paul, *Le Romant comique*, ed. H. Bénac, Paris, Société des Belles-Lettres (Les Textes Français), 1951, 2 vols. Contains a very full and perceptive introduction. Original spelling.
3. ——, *Le Roman comique*, ed. E. Magne, Paris, Garnier Frères (Classiques Garnier), 1955. Modernized spelling; reproduces the *Suite d'Offray*.
4. ——, *Le Roman comique*, ed. Y. Giraud, Paris, Garnier-Flammarion, 1981. Useful paperback edition, with good introduction and notes.
5. ——, *Le Roman comique*, ed. J. Serroy, Paris, Gallimard (Folio), 1985. As above, with in addition analysis of and extracts from all the continuations.
6. Sorel, Charles, *Histoire comique de Francion*, ed. Y. Giraud, Paris, Garnier-Flammarion, 1979.
7. Furetière, Antoine, *Le Roman bourgeois*, ed. J. Prévot, Paris, Gallimard (Folio), 1981.

OTHER PRIMARY TEXTS

8. Boileau, Nicolas, *Satires*, in *Œuvres*, Paris, Garnier Frères (Classiques Garnier), 1961.
9. Corneille, Pierre, *L'Illusion comique*, in *Œuvres complètes*, Paris, Seuil (L'Intégrale), 1963.
10. Gide, André, *Les Faux-Monnayeurs*, in *Romans*, Paris, Gallimard (Bibliothèque de la Pléiade), 1958.
11. ——, *Journal des Faux-Monnayeurs*, Paris, Gallimard, 1927.
12. Mallarmé, Stéphane, *Œuvres complètes*, Paris, Gallimard (Bibliothèque de la Pléiade), 1945.

13. Rabelais, François, *Le Quart Livre*, in *Œuvres complètes*, Paris, Garnier Frères (Classiques Garnier), 1962, 2 volumes, Vol. 2.
14. Sorel, Charles, *Le Berger extravagant*, Paris, T. du Bray, 1627, 6 volumes.
15. ——, *La Bibliothèque françoise*, [Paris, 1664], Geneva, Slatkine Reprints, 1970.

BROADER CRITICAL WORKS, WORKS ON THE FRENCH NOVEL AND WORKS ON LITERATURE IN THE SEVENTEENTH CENTURY

16. Adam, A., *Les Libertins au XVIIe siècle*, Paris, Buchet-Chastel, 1964. Selection of texts with commentary.
17. Bardon, M., *Don Quichotte en France au XVIIe et XVIIIe siècles*, Paris, Champion, 1931. Dated, but not superseded.
18. Booth, W., 'The self-conscious narrator in comic fiction before *Tristram Shandy*', *PMLA*, 67 (1952), pp.163-85. A useful brief survey.
19. Chédozeau, B., *Le Baroque*, Paris, Nathan, 1989. More up-to-date and broader in its reference than Rousset.
20. Coulet, H., *Le Roman jusqu'à la Révolution*, Paris, Armand Colin, 1967. Magisterial and eminently readable survey of the genre.
21. Cronk, N., 'La défense du dialogisme: vers une poétique du burlesque' in *Burlesque et formes parodiques*, ed. I. Landy-Houillon and M. Ménard, Tübingen (*PFSCL*), 1987, pp.293-318. Contains helpful definitions.
22. Forster, E.M., *Aspects of the novel*, ed. O. Stallybrass, London, Penguin, 1974.
23. Hainsworth, G., *'Las Novelas ejemplares' de Cervantès en France au XVIIe siècle*, Paris, Champion, 1933. Detailed and scholarly.
24. Hodgson, R., 'The parody of traditional narrative structures in the French anti-novel from Charles Sorel to Diderot', *Neophilologus*, 66 (1982), pp.340-48.
25. LeBreton, A., *Le Roman au XVIIe siècle*, Paris, Hachette, n.d. For a long time the best general survey; now somewhat out of date.
26. Lever, M., *Le Roman français au XVIIe siècle*, Paris, PUF, 1981. Excellent sharp, modern and succinct survey of the genre in the period; revised and expanded edition published by Fayard in 1996 under the title *Romanciers du Grand Siècle*.
27. Mallinson, G.J., 'Fiction, morality and the reader: reflections on the classical formula *plaire et instruire*', *Continuum*, 1 (1989), pp.203-28.
28. Muratore, M.-J., *Mimesis and metatextuality in the French neo-classical text*, Geneva, Droz, 1994. Provocative but excessively ungenerous in its reading of Scarron.

114 _Le Roman comique_

29. Orr, L., *Problems and poetics of the nonaristotelian novel*, Lewisburg, Bucknell University Press, 1986. Wide-ranging if somewhat technical.
30. Reynier, G., *Le Roman réaliste au XVIIe siècle*, Paris, A. Colin, 1914. Dated.
31. Rousset, J., *La Littérature de l'âge baroque en France*, Paris, Corti, 1963. An authoritative work in its day, in part superseded by Chédozeau.
32. Serroy, J., *Roman et réalité: les histoires comiques au XVIIe siècle*, Grenoble, Presses Universitaires de Grenoble, 1980. Remains the standard and most thorough scholarly work on the comic sub-genre.
33. Waugh, Patricia, *Metafiction: the theory and practice of self-conscious fiction*, London, Methuen, 1984. Occasionally difficult, but clear and instructive by its (implicit) applicability to Scarron.

WORKS SPECIFICALLY OR PRINCIPALLY DEVOTED TO THE ROMAN COMIQUE

34. Alter, J., 'L'Être et le paraître dans le *Roman comique*', *L'Esprit Créateur*, 13 (1973), pp.183-95.
35. Cadorel, R., 'Les nouvelles espagnoles du *Roman comique*', *Revue de littérature comparée*, 36 (1962), pp.244-52. An exhaustive study of the Spanish intertexts.
36. De Armas, F., *Paul Scarron*, New York, Twayne Publishers Inc. (Twayne's World Authors Series, 194), 1972. Strong on the Spanish background (see also 45 below), though over-concerned to identify a moral dimension.
37. ———, *The four interpolated stories in the 'Roman comique'*, Chapel Hill, University of North Carolina Press, 1971.
38. Dédéyan, C., *Le 'Roman comique' de Scarron*, Paris, Société d'édition et d'enseignement supérieur, 1983. Some useful information; better on evidence than interpretation.
39. DeJean, J., *Scarron's 'Roman comique': a comedy of the novel, a novel of comedy*, Bern, Peter Lang, 1977. Modern, energetic and challenging, if occasionally inaccurate.
40. Mariani, G., *La condizione dell'uomo di teatro nel 'Romant comique' di Scarron*, Florence, La Nuova Italia Editrice, 1973. The best survey of the theatrical context. (In Italian.)
41. Ménard, M., 'Les illustrations du *Roman comique* de Scarron par J.-B. Coulom' in *Burlesques et formes parodiques*, ed. I. Landy-Houillon and M. Ménard, Tübingen (PFSCL), 1976, pp.293-318.
42. Mortier, R., 'La fonction des nouvelles dans *Le Roman comique*', *CAIEF*, 18 (1986), pp.41-51.

43. Parish, R., 'Scarron's *Roman comique*: contradictions and terms', *Seventeenth-Century French Studies*, 16 (1994), pp.105-18.
44. Rousset, J., 'Insertions et interventions dans *Le Roman comique*', *L'Esprit Créateur*, 11 (1971), 141-53. Modern and careful, if slightly laboured.
45. Simon, E., 'The function of the Spanish stories in Scarron's *Roman comique*', *L'Esprit Créateur*, 3 (1963), 130-36. Attractively argued, and broader in range than the title would suggest.

TRANSLATION

46. Scarron, Paul, *The Comic Romance, translated by Tom Brown et al.,* 1700, ed. B. Boyce, New York and London, Benjamin Blom, 1968.

CRITICAL GUIDES TO FRENCH TEXTS

edited by

Roger Little, Wolfgang van Emden, David Williams

68. **Simon Davies**. Laclos: Les Liaisons dangereuses
69. **Keith Beaumont**. Jarry: Ubu Roi
70. **G.J. Mallinson**. Molière: L'Avare
71. **Susan Taylor-Horrex**. Verlaine: Fêtes galantes *and* Romances
    sans paroles
72. **Malcolm Cook**. Lesage: Gil Blas
73. **Sheila Bell**. Sarraute: Portrait d'un inconnu *and* Vous les
    entendez?
74. **W.D. Howarth**. Corneille: Le Cid
75. **Peter Jimack**. Diderot: Supplément au Voyage de Bougainville
76. **Christopher Lloyd**. Maupassant: Bel-Ami
77. **David H. Walker**. Gide: Les Nourritures terrestres *and*
    La Symphonie pastorale
78. **Noël Peacock**. Molière: Les Femmes savantes
79. **Jean H. Duffy**. Butor: La Modification
80. **J.P. Little**. Genet: Les Nègres
81. **John Campbell**. Racine: Britannicus
82. **Malcolm Quainton**. D'Aubigné: Les Tragiques
83. **Henry Phillips**. Racine: Mithridate
84. **S. Beynon John**. Saint-Exupéry: Vol de nuit *and* Terre des
    hommes
85. **John Trethewey**. Corneille: L'Illusion comique *and* Le Menteur
86. **John Dunkley**. Beaumarchais: Le Barbier de Séville
87. **Valerie Minogue**. Zola: L'Assommoir
88. **Kathleen Hall**. Rabelais: Pantagruel *and* Gargantua
89. **A.W. Raitt**. Flaubert: Trois contes
90. **Toby Garfitt**. Mauriac: Thérèse Desqueyroux
91. **Margaret M. Callander**. Colette: Le Blé en herbe *and* La Chatte
92. **David Whitton**. Molière: Le Bourgeois gentilhomme
93. **Peter Cogman**. Mérimée: Colomba *and* Carmen
94. **Derek A. Watts**. Corneille: Rodogune *and* Nicomède
95. **Russell Cousins**. Zola: Thérèse Raquin
96. **David Coward**. Pagnol: La Gloire de mon père *and* Le Château
    de ma mère
97. **Kathleen M. McKilligan**. Mauriac: Le Nœud de vipères
98. **Keith Busby**. Chrétien de Troyes: Perceval (Le Conte du Graal)
99. **Renate Günther**. Duras: Le Ravissement de Lol V. Stein *and*
    L'Amant
100. **R.A. Francis**. Prévost: Manon Lescaut